PELICAN BOOKS

EUROPEAN PAINTING AND SCULPTURE

BY
ERIC NEWTON

(A 82)

PELICAN BOOKS

EUROPEAN PAINTING
AND SCULPTURE

BY
ERIC NEWTON

Published by
PENGUIN BOOKS

HARMONDSWORTH MIDDLESEX ENGLAND
245 FIFTH AVENUE NEW YORK U.S.A.

First Published 1941
Second Edition January 1942
Third Edition November, 1945

FOR
STELLA MARY

MADE AND PRINTED IN GREAT BRITAIN FOR PENGUIN BOOKS LIMITED
BY HUNT, BARNARD AND CO., LTD., LONDON AND AYLESBURY

CONTENTS

ACKNOWLEDGMENTS

Acknowledgment is made for the use of the following illustrations:

The Guitar Lesson, by Terborch; *Martyrdom of St. Sebastian*, by Pollaiuolo; *The Lock*, by Constable; *Philip IV When Young*, by Velasquez; *Mountain View*; *Statue of Kha-Em-Uast*. Mansell photographs.

Burial of Count Orgaz, by Greco; *Self Portrait of Rembrandt*; *La Notte*, by Michelangelo; *Venus*, by Titian; *Descent from the Cross*, by Giotto. Anderson photographs.

Rouen Cathedral, by Monet; *The Crucifixion*, by Grünewald. Bulloz photographs.

Chartres Cathedral. A Neurdein photograph.

Toilette de la Mariée, by Courbet. A Bernheim Jeune photograph.

Still Life, by Picasso. A Paul Rosenberg photograph.

Assumption of the Virgin, by Rubens. An E. & S. photograph.

FOREWORD

WHAT! Another history of art?

Yes. Why not? History is not a finite thing. Nor is art an absolute thing. The facts at every art historian's disposal are the same, but his selection of them and his interpretation of them must always depend on himself. I am certain that the facts that seem to me important are not quite the same as those that have seemed important to previous writers. And if some of them are the same, I am certain that the conclusions I shall draw from them will be different. The historian-critic sees art very much as the artist sees nature. No two artists see nature and no two critics see art from the same angle.

Moreover, I have very definite ideas as to the purpose to be served by a history of art. I have a feeling that out of a hundred people who know quite a lot about pictures and statues not half a dozen know what painting and sculpture really are. They think of the Mona Lisa and the Elgin Marbles as beautiful things, things to be looked at and admired and perhaps (if art is their "subject") studied. But they do not think of them as transmitters and of themselves as receivers.

My hope in writing this book is to turn a few admirers into receivers: not to describe pictures and statues or to relate facts about them so much as to induce my readers to tune in to painting and sculpture in whatever form they may manifest themselves, at whatever period or in whatever country. And I can only do that by giving an account of the working of my own receiving set. I do not pretend that it is an exceptional receiving set. On some wave-lengths, I am ashamed to say, it gives me rather poor results. When that happens the reader will at once be aware that something has gone wrong. He will notice patches in this book in which the reception is dull and blurred. They may perhaps stimulate him to a higher pitch of sensitiveness than I am capable of myself. In that case even the dull patches will not have been written in vain.

This is not a student's book. For persons with an appetite for facts there is an abundance of reference books. I have not hesitated to draw upon them myself. I have not seen Rembrandt's birth certificate with my own eyes. I do not even care whether it exists, but I believe that eminent scholar, Dr. Z., when he tells me that Rembrandt was born in 1606. To him and countless other authorities I am indebted for such facts as appear in the following pages.

For my opinions, on the other hand, I am indebted to no one. It is not the ingredients but the flavour of paintings and carvings that I have tried to communicate. If I have failed to do that it must be for one of two reasons. My palate may be to blame; or the distressing fact that a flavour, like a tune, can never be accurately described in words.

Nevertheless paintings and sculptures are not quite like tunes. They seem to me to be . . . but what they seem to me to be is set forth in my first two chapters, which were written in order to clear the ground for the history that follows. The reader who feels that the ground needs no clearing can profitably skip them and turn at once to chapter three.

CHAPTER I

THE NATURE OF THE ARTS

A POSTAGE stamp, the overture to the Magic Flute, No. 7, Acacia Grove, Guerlain's latest perfume, Leonardo's "Last Supper," an innings by Don Bradman, Shakespeare's "Hamlet," a performance of "Sylphides," a dish of "homard à la cardinal," St. Paul's Cathedral, a Walt Disney cartoon—all these are (or can be) works of art.

There are other things that are not works of art. Niagara Falls is not a work of art, nor is the afterglow of the snows of Monte Rosa, nor the sound of breakers against a cliff, nor the dance executed by washing hanging on a clothes line in a stiff breeze, nor the scent of a pine wood on a summer day.

These two classes of phenomena are different in kind. The first are man-made and man-designed. They had to be conceived in the mind of a man (or group of men) and then made communicable to other men by the skill of the designer, working in some medium that could be perceived by the senses of other men—the eye, the ear, the nose, the palate.

The other set of phenomena—Niagara Falls, the sound of breakers and so on—are not man-made or man-designed. They may be equally beautiful or equally pleasurable. They may even be the result of design by God or the Laws of Nature or what you will, but they have not that double element in them of conception and parturition. They were not imagined first and then made manifest through the medium of visible materials, visible movements, audible sounds, perceptible smells.

Art has always fascinated the makers of definitions, and has always baffled them; the makers of definitions are never content to define what a thing *is*: they usually attempt to describe what it is *for*. And though I myself have no doubt at all about what art *is*, no sequence of words known to me will describe what art is *for*.

In trying to tell the story of art I shall therefore start with an initial advantage. I have no preconceived theories about the artist's purpose: therefore I have no prejudice against the artist who runs counter to such theories. If the artist tells me a story

I shall exclaim "how interesting!"; if he wishes to overawe me with mystical conceptions of the Godhead I am ready to be impressed: if he wants to construct a purely formal pattern of line and colour or mass or sound, I will say "how beautiful!": if he preaches I am ready to be converted: if he wants to be of use to me I shall say "thank you." Art has done all these things at various times in the history of civilization.

But if the story of art is to be told it is certainly necessary to know what art is, and if I define it briefly as a human conception made manifest by the use of a medium: and if I define good art (and no one wants to waste his time telling the story of bad art) as a noble (or arresting, or interesting, or valuable) conception made manifest by the skilful use of a medium, I can then have done with definitions and get on with the story.

This is not the history of the whole family of the arts. It is merely an outline of the story of two members of that family— painting and sculpture. Rather odd members, as we shall see later. Curiously different from their next-of-kin in many ways and for that reason generally misunderstood. But conscientious biographers should start with an introductory chapter on their hero's family and pedigree, and this brief chapter is an attempt to state the case for the arts as a whole.

The artist, then, is a man of double activity. He has to have imagination and he has to have craftsmanship. He has to imagine (in his mind's eye, or his mind's ear, or his mind's nose) the thing he is going to make: and he must also have the power to translate the thing he has imagined into terms of his medium. Those are not separate activities. On the contrary, they affect one another in unpredictable and unanalysable ways, so that when an artist is at work he cannot possibly say at a given moment which part of himself he is using. Is the fact that he is working with a soft pencil on rough paper giving a breadth to Tintoretto's line, or had the image in his mind's eye already formed itself with that breadth of sweep? Did Mozart, in his mind's ear, conjure up a quality of sound that could only be translated into music by a certain combination of bassoons and strings? Or did his memory of that combination, heard perhaps by chance while an orchestra was tuning up, prompt him to make further experiments with it? No one can possibly answer these questions, since no one but Tintoretto himself knew the precise quality of the image in his mind's eye and no one but Mozart ever heard what was in Mozart's mind's ear. The work of art, the drawing or the overture, is all we have to judge by. We can only say, "this man *seems* to have found an adequate means of expression for the thing he had to say." A marriage has taken place between the visionary and the craftsman and one can only judge of the success of the marriage by examining the fruits of it—the work of art.

But this artistic activity—this making of drawings and overtures and books and postage stamps is not a thing done just for the fun of doing it. No doubt it *is* fun to write a book or compose an overture, but no artist was ever content to have his fun and then throw the result of it away. The book has to be read, the overture performed, the ballet or picture seen. Art is a communication. Behind every work of art is the artist's appeal to his fellows, "Don't you see what I mean? Don't you see what I'm getting at?"

The story of art is therefore not merely the story of men who make things and of the kind of things they make. It is also the story of the relationship—the very complicated and always shifting relationship—between these men and their fellow men. It is a relationship full of contradictions and difficulties. For no workman can afford to produce unless he is paid to do so; therefore the artist has to have an employer. And no employer can afford to pay a workman unless he is producing something that he (the employer) needs. It follows therefore that (except in the rare case of artists of independent means) the artist's work of art is not merely the child of his own personal fancy, the thing he personally wants to communicate. It must also be something that his employer wants him to communicate to himself or to others. The work of art must be not only the result of an urge on the part of the producer, but also of a need on the part of the consumer. Here is a strange state of things indeed! For how can the consumer feel a need of something so personal and so (on the face of it) unnecessary as an artist's expression of his inner vision? And even supposing he does feel that need sufficiently strongly to induce him to pay an artist to produce a work of art, how is the artist going to reconcile his personal and private desire to communicate his own personal and private vision with his employer's or patron's specification of what he wants the artist to produce? In any other branch of human activity the question would not arise. No maker of chisels would say to his employer, "My whole nature rebels against the idea of making the kind of chisels you want. You wish me to make sharp chisels. I, on the other hand, can only express myself to the full by making blunt chisels. You want steel chisels; I, as a craftsman, feel irresistibly drawn to the use of lead as medium."

The more materially useful a man-made thing is, the more chance there is of complete agreement between artist and employer. But material usefulness is not the only kind of usefulness: there is such a thing as spiritual usefulness. To the maker of chisels the employer can justifiably say, "Make your chisels exactly thus," but to the maker of crucifixes he must say, "Let your crucifix conform to the minimum requirements of all crucifixes—a cross, a male human body, an impression of suffering, but also a sense of nobility. Beyond that I leave it to you. Add your own personal thoughts and feelings. Embody your own vision."

So as long as the artist is an employed workman he must compromise, never losing touch with life and its requirements yet never sacrificing his own integrity in doing so. And that is almost always a good thing, for compromise of that kind is not a concession to a lower order of things. It is a dangerous holding of the balance between two sets of forces. The artist, like the maker of chisels, serves a master (Palestrina served the Pope, Shakespeare wrote his plays for a touring company), but in doing so he gives his master something he never bargained for. When Rembrandt painted the "Night Watch" he was ostensibly painting the portraits of a certain Captain Banning Cocq and the members of his shooting company. Presumably something corresponding to a group photograph of the school hockey team would have satisfied the club, but Rembrandt had things to say that had nothing to do with the likenesses of the captain and his friends—things about how light falls in dark places, and how it strikes hard here and gently caresses there —and he insisted on saying them. In doing so he began to lose sight of the original purpose of his picture. Banning Cocq and his friends became mere excuses for an essay in chiaroscuro. The club was offended; certain members of it complained that their faces had been plunged into semi-darkness; they were more interested in themselves than in chiaroscuro. We, on the other hand, are delighted. We have lost interest in seventeenth-century shooting clubs, but what Rembrandt has to say about the play of light on flesh is as fascinating to-day as it was in 1642. A similar controversy, it will be remembered, arose a few years ago in connection with the statue of Sir Douglas Haig in Whitehall. Michelangelo, faced with the same kind of criticism of his statues of Lorenzo and Giuliano de Medici, answered that in a thousand years' time nobody would know what the two Medicis were really like. Pope Clement VII, however, who ordered the statues, *did* know; he asked for portraits of two men and he was given symbols of mankind. Michelangelo was unwilling to make the compromise. We may be glad of his unwillingness, but his employer was anything but pleased.

This necessity of serving two masters has always been one of the artist's difficulties. He must deliver the goods he is asked for, and he must also be true to himself. And rightly so. Whenever either is sacrificed to the other the work of art suffers in quality. There are plenty of instances of both kinds of sacrifice in the art of to-day. There are commercial artists who produce flavourless trash in an attempt to give their employers what they want: and there are artists who, through lack of employers or through unwillingness to be employed, have nothing to serve but their own impulses, and whose work can only be described as psychological exhibitionism.

It is not by chance that the greatest periods of art have usually occurred when the artist was most firmly harnessed to a master or to a cause. Necessarily the pace of a man in harness is slower than that of a free man. He is less free to choose his own direction, but he has the satisfaction of knowing that he is an indispensable member of society—or of a portion of society—and the further satisfaction of knowing that because society needs him, society will understand him—at any rate that portion of him that is in service. His double service gives him a double message and a double appeal. A Palestrina, left to himself, will merely further the cause of music: employed by the Pope, he also enriches the texture of Christian ritual and enlarges the meaning of Christianity.

The present-day cleavage of artists into two groups, those who are enslaved to their employers that they "can't call their souls their own," and those unfettered spirits whose souls are so much their own that they are no use to anyone but themselves, is a comparatively new thing. It has led to the division of artists into two kinds known as "commercial" and "fine artists"—i.e. men who only work to please the man who pays them and men who have no one to please but themselves—though these latter always hope that they will happen to please someone else sufficiently to induce him to pay them enough to go on pleasing themselves without starving. Three-quarters of the films made, about a quarter of the books published, ninety per cent. of the music composed are "commercial" in the true sense that they were created primarily in order to be turned into money. The bulk of the remainder, the "fine" works of art, are genuine attempts at self expression without reference to the requirements of society. In some cases they succeed so well in impressing themselves on society that society begins to require them. In others they are so personal and so remote from average human experience that society, far from requiring them, complains of their uselessness, their unintelligibility, their divorce from "life." That complaint, so often heard nowadays, is not a criterion of the genuineness or sincerity of the works of art in question. It is an index of the unfamiliarity of the language in which those works of art are couched. For a personal vision demands a personal set of idioms to express it. Usually a generation or so must pass before those idioms become understood and accepted by the average man and pass into general currency. The time-lag between the appearance of an unfamiliar artistic message couched in an unfamiliar artistic idiom, and its acceptance by the average man can only be reduced when the artist can be harnessed to a cause that the average man understands. Giotto was as violent an innovator as Picasso, but as Giotto's innovations were harnessed to Christianity (while Picasso's are harnessed to nothing more stable than Picasso) the average contemporary of Giotto, shocked though he may have been by the new Giottesque idiom, felt that he could at least understand the cause that idiom served, and could dimly see how the new idiom somehow served the cause in a new and valuable way. To-day the same phenomenon can be observed. The more the artist is willing to compromise between making what *he* wants (in Rembrandt's case, a study of light) and what his employer wants (in Banning Cocq's case a set of recognizable portraits) the more immediately acceptable his work will be. A cubist whose picture conveys nothing but the cubiness of things in general is apt to leave the average man cold and puzzled. But a cubist who uses his cubism to advertise the merits of A's petrol or B's beer is understood at once. A cubized egg is, to the average man, simply a bad egg; but a cubized glass of beer grasped in a cubized hand is interesting and arresting. The one is merely an artist's visual adventure, the other is a voyage of discovery that carries the spectator along with it and deposits him surprisingly at his destination. Once the artist has harnessed himself to society, society at once begins to regard him as a workman performing a useful function and not as a playboy amusing himself in a vacuum.

In the same way a scientist's discovery that an electric current passed through metal coil will heat the metal leaves most people uninterested, but the man who uses that discovery to boil a kettle arouses an immediate interest.

This double function of the artist is the key to the story of art. Many learned books about art have been written which fail to tell the story because they lose sight of the perpetual adjustment that goes on in the artist between art-as-expression and art-as-service.

Meanwhile before going on to examine the particular kind of adjustments that take place when the artist happens to be a painter or a sculptor, one other thing must be said about the arts in general A work of art may be an expression of the artist's inner vision, and it may also be a thing useful to society, but beyond both these it is a thing-in-itself. Apart from its function as a means of communion between one human being and another it exists in its own right. It consists of a series of sounds or words or movements or of a set of shapes made of pigment applied to canvas or of a set of masses carved out of stone or modelled out of clay. In a word, it has form: and it must obey the laws of form as dictated by whatever medium the artist uses. A sentence may embody an idea in the writer's mind, but it must also obey grammatical laws. A drawing may say what the draughtsman wanted it to say but it must also say it in the pencil's way. A statue may represent a man in a lounge suit, but, if it is made of stone, both flesh and cloth must be translated into terms of stone: stone must not be tortured into an imitation of flesh and cloth. Every medium has its own set of laws, and the work of art must obey them or perish. When the word is made flesh it ceases to have the qualities of word-ness. It must behave like flesh.

Moreover, the work of art is self-contained. A picture must have four edges, a play or piece of music must have a beginning and an end, whereas the experience it embodies has no edges, no beginning or end. It is just an indeterminate slice of an endless ebb and flow. But the work of art must be a thing that can be isolated from all surrounding things. A picture occupies a square yard of space, a symphony three-quarters of an hour of time, a play several cubic yards of space and a couple of hours of time. Having "edges," therefore, in space or time, it follows that it must also have a shape. E. M. Forster, in his remarkable essay on the novel, points out that Anatole France's "Thaïs" is shaped like an hour-glass. ("We do not see it as an hour-glass—that is the hard jargon of the lecture room—but if it was not for this hour-glass the story, the plot and the characters of Thaïs and Paphnuce would none of them exert their full force, they would none of them breathe as they do.") Percy Lubbock's "Roman Pictures" is shaped like a "grand chain." ("What is so good in 'Roman Pictures' is not the presence of the 'grand chain' pattern—anyone can organize a grand chain—but the suitability of the pattern to the author's mood.") Observe the word pattern. The arts are difficult things to write about because there is no adequate terminology that fits them all. "Pattern" is a work taken from graphic art, "rhythm" from music, "phrasing" from literature. But they all have their counterparts in each other and they have all been invented by people who want (as I do) to talk about the work of art as a thing-in-itself, a thing with form, as opposed to a thing with content. Pattern, for example, is visual rhythm; a set of relationships set up in the eye of the beholder. A drawing of a flower is just a drawing of a flower, a thing that imparts a certain amount of botanical information. But repeat that drawing three times side by side on a square of paper and you have a pattern. You have established a relationship between three things and not only between three things but also between them and the four edges of the paper, and that relationship can be pleasant or unpleasant without any reference to botany. As long as a work of art has a shape it must also have a pattern. Pattern is a subdivision of shape. The parts within the shape must be related to the shape and to each other.

The artist's feeling for form and shape has given birth, in all the arts, to a host of conventions that are on the face of them fantastic. Why should poets have invented a shape called the sonnet? Why should the ear have to be tickled with an elaborate system of rhymes? What is the virtue of fourteen iambic pentameters if thirteen or fifteen would equally well express the poet's thought? Why should Edward Lear, in recounting the brief but poignant story of the old man of Aosta, have decided to fit his story into the strange shape of a Limerick with its attendant pattern of lines —long, long, short, short, long—and its parallel pattern of rhymes—a, a, b, b, a? What gave birth to the Sonata form? One can only answer that deep down in manking is a thirst for something we have agreed to call æsthetic pleasure, a thirst for order, harmony, balance, rhythm, pattern.

Each art has its own set of conventions, but this brief chapter is not the place to examine them in detail. Those that apply to painting and sculpture will be considered in the next chapter. Meanwhile it is sufficient to remember that the artist, in the act of creation, is perpetually obsessed with this question of the form his work of art is taking. His picture is not merely a representation of an object, or an expression of his feeling about an object. It is a thing-in-itself, equally valid if it is turned upside down: equally valid if it is an inaccurate representation, or a representation of something that lies outside the spectator's experience (as, say, a picture of a snow scene would be to an inhabitant of the Sahara desert): a thing that justifies itself by its shape alone and the obedience of that shape to the laws of the medium in which it is made.

CHAPTER II

THE REPRESENTATIONAL ARTS

So much for works of art as a whole. They communicate their maker's message in terms of a medium: they serve society: they have form and all the odd attributes that the word "form" implies; and their form must not contradict the nature of the medium in which they are made.

This book is about painting and sculpture; and this chapter is about the special laws that govern the painting of pictures and the making of statues. In what way do these two differ from the other arts?

The first thing that occurs to one is that they are both capable of representing objects known to or imagined by their creators. They *need* not do so, of course. There are sculptors and painters to-day whose carvings and pictures do not represent known objects. But on the whole it has been the practice of painters and sculptors to produce works of which one could say, "Look! that is a man; there is a tree and a bank of cloud; that is surely a statue of the goddess Venus." And, in case of doubt, pictures and statues usually have titles to help one to identify the object represented. These titles are not an integral part of the work of art, though they may cause disturbance in the mind of the spectator when taken in conjunction with the work of art. A picture of a fat priest surrounded by hens may please the spectator immensely until he finds that it is called "St. Francis preaching to the birds." Whereupon his pleasure is modified and may turn to puzzlement or even disgust. But what really puzzles and disgusts him is not the picture but the relation between the picture and the title. On the whole, however, titles are there to eliminate puzzlement. "No. 27, Hampstead Heath" in the catalogue simply means, "Don't waste time wondering what part of the country this landscape represents. It is a picture of Hampstead Heath. Now you can enjoy it as a picture."

This sort of thing doesn't happen with the other arts. Literature can describe but it cannot represent. Music uses representation (I mean the representation of audible things, like the baa-ing of the sheep in Strauss's "Don Quixote" or the nightingale's song in Beethoven's Pastoral Symphony) so rarely that musical representation need not be taken into account. But painting *can* be entirely dependent on representation, so that a passage in any picture which cannot be identified as a known object may become a source of irritation to the spectator.

Painting and sculpture therefore differ from the other arts in that they are, in the main, representational arts. But if that were all that could be said about them the affair would be simple. The most accurate possible representation of, say, a man, would be the best work of art; the climax of portraiture would be the wax-work. The object of painting and sculpture would be to deceive the eye, and since sculpture is three-dimensional while painting is only two-dimensional, sculpture would be the greater art of the two. Madame Tussaud's would contain more masterpieces than the National Portrait Gallery.

Such a theory is manifestly absurd, because it leaves out of account all that we have already found to be common to all the arts. A waxwork does not communicate a message. Or rather its message is so simple ("this is what So-and-so looks like") that it can be ignored. It serves no special need except that of idle curiosity. Its form is not created in the interests of shape or pattern or harmony of mass and colour. It is not a thing-in-itself. It is merely a copy of a thing already in existence. It may be work of extraordinary skill, but it is not a work of art.

And yet the will to represent is part of the average painter's or sculptor's creative make-up and the desire to recognise his representation is equally part of the average spectator's. If we define art as the communication of a conception in terms of a medium, we must define painting as the communication of a visual conception in terms of paint. And since most visual conceptions are based on the memory of the appearance of natural objects, the painter will usually end up by painting pictures of *things*. Admittedly his picture will be a set of references to actual appearances, but its *raison d'être* will not be to impart information about appearances. That is the camera's job. The painter must use those references to communicate his message and he must impose form upon them however unwilling they may be to accept such an imposition.

At once it becomes clear that in painting and sculpture we have to do with two rather clumsy, unmanageable members of the art family. Music can be poured into any mould. The mind's ear is free to conceive any set of rhythms, any sequence of sounds or qualities of sound in any degree of loudness. But in painting the artist it tied down by a set of obligations—obligations to the *appearance* of things, the shapes, colours and sizes of things—which are almost certain to conflict with his sense of form. A painting "about" something (whether it be "about" the assassination of Julius Caesar or a couple of onions and a glass of water) cannot also be whole-heartedly "about" the purely formal set of values that music takes as its starting point. Nor can it even be quite whole-heartedly "about" the more permanent and universal side of the artist's visual experience. As I said in the last chapter, a Rembrandt, painting the "Night Watch," is torn between producing a set of likenesses of certain gentlemen of Amsterdam, and painting the play of light on a complex series of surfaces. To Rembrandt, the painter of light and shadow, it is irrelevant that those surfaces are the faces, hands and clothing of Banning Cocq and his friends. To Rembrandt the portrait painter the play of light is of little consequence. But to Rembrandt the master of *form*, the *designer*, both likeness and play of light are of no consequence whatever. He is concerned with covering an area of canvas with pigment in such a way that the disposition of lights and darks (*not* lights and *shadows*), of colours and lines, is pleasing to the eye. He is doing exactly the same thing as the composer who fills in a section of time with a disposition of sounds, rhythms, timbres, etc., in such a way as to please the ear. From the point of view of form the only difference between a painting and a piece of music is that the one occupies space, the other time. Both are decorations, existing only in their own right and existing only to satisfy the innate hunger of the eye and the ear for formal harmony.

What distinguishes the painter's problem from the composer's is that whereas music is a formalized expression of what is in the composer's mind's ear, the picture is a formalized expression of what is in the painter's mind's eye *plus* a recognizable representation of certain objects. The painter, instead of serving two masters, has to serve three—expression, form and representation. The result of this threefold obligation is a splitting of loyalties on the part of the painter which only the greatest artists have been able to survive: and a confusion of mind on the part of the spectator which has led to endless misunderstanding. If it were not for this particular complexity, I should not have considered it necessary to preface a history of art with a philosophy of art.

*   *   *   *   *

Imagine an artist commissioned to paint an altarpiece of a Madonna and Child in a space of a certain shape and size.

He has four jobs to do, three as an artist and one as a craftsman.

(1) He has to invent a set of shapes and colours which will express his feeling about the Madonna-and-Child theme.

(2) He has to invent a set of shapes and colours which will (however vaguely) remind the spectator of a woman holding a baby.

(3) He has to invent a set of shapes and colours which will fill the required space pleasantly, and

(4) Having reconciled the conflicting claims of these three sets of inventions, he has to translate them into pigment applied to a flat surface.

The difficulties of reconciling 1, 2 and 3 are, of course enormous. Take job No. 1. The Madonna-and-Child theme is a purely emotional affair. What he has to express, put in its simplest terms, is a certain kind of tenderness, motherliness, and sympathy, together with a sense of divinity. Now tenderness, motherliness, sympathy and divinity are feelings, and feelings have no shape, colour, size or pattern. And yet the artist can only express himself in terms of shapes, colours and patterns. Job No. 1 is therefore to invent a set of shapes and colours which will *suggest* to the spectator feelings of tenderness and motherliness and divinity. These shapes and colours are not, and cannot be, representations; they are equivalents or symbols.

Job No. 2 is easy in itself. Almost anyone with good eyesight and a trained visual memory (or even without one, since models can be hired for a few shillings an hour) can conjure up in his mind's eye an image of a woman and a baby; and almost anyone, after a year or so of determined effort, can learn to turn that image into paint so that the picture will look rather like his woman-and-baby image. There have been certain primitive peoples who couldn't have done it if they had tried (though it would never have occurred to them to try), but certainly any European painter from the year 1500 onwards could have painted a woman holding a baby skilfully enough to leave the spectator in no doubt as to what the woman looked like, what the baby looked like, how the woman was holding the baby, what sort of clothes they were both wearing and so on. Yes, job No. 2 is easy enough. The difficulty is to reconcile it with job No. 1. To paint a picture of divine motherly tenderness, free from the bonds of space and time, and also to paint a picture of two persons with particular features and expressions, in a particular light and particular setting. Manifestly the thing is impossible. A compromise must be found. But half the virtue of art lies in its power to compromise. The conflicting claims in painting of symbolism and representation are very like the conflicting claims in life of body and soul. And just as the finest forms of life are neither the extremes of hedonism on the one hand or of asceticism on the other, but a balance of the two, so the finest kind of painting is neither pure representation nor pure symbolism but a reconciliation of the two.

Job No. 3 is the artist's basic job, but, alas, it is one that cannot be adequately written about. The formal relationship of the parts of a work of art to each other and to the whole work can be understood only by the particular sense to which the work addresses itself. Visual form is a matter on which the eye alone can arbitrate. Figures 3, 4, 5 and 6 show four Madonna-and-Child pictures; in each case it is easy enough to point out what sacrifices have been made in effecting the adjustment between the symbolized idea and the represented object. The Russian ikon takes symbolism just about as far as it can reasonably go and cheerfully sacrifices visual truth about women and children to symbolic truth about tenderness and divinity. Simone makes further concessions to appearances, and in doing so allows the emotional temperature to drop a little. Raphael insists on the solidity of his figures and on placing them in a landscape instead of the idealized space symbolized by Simone's gold background. Raphael's idea of a picture is a view seen through a hole cut in the wall. Simone's is a decoration painted on the wall. Consequently instead of a symbol of Madonnahood he has made a representation of a Madonna. The symbol of tenderness has given place to a portrait of a woman behaving tenderly. Finally, Tiepolo takes the progression from symbol to representation one stage further. The symbol has now been ousted by the representation. We are given a charming portrait of a lovely signora and her exceptionally fine child. The clouds that conceal the model's throne deceive no one. The artist who thinks that by the addition of a cloud he can turn a portrait into a religious picture knows very little about religion. His picture may be an adequate expression of his own inner vision of motherhood, but as a piece of social service, as an example of Christian propaganda, it is a lamentable failure.

This interplay between symbolism and representation is easy enough to describe in words. It is a phenomenon that can be readily grasped by the mind. Both symbolism and representation are references to human experience, and any man with a well-stocked experience can understand them. Whoever knows the meaning of the word "tenderness" cannot fail to recognise that the Russian ikon painter has discovered an adequate equivalent for it in paint. And whoever knows what a beautiful woman and a well-nourished baby look like must admit that Tiepolo has made an adequate pictorial representation of them. But when the critic or historian comes to assess or describe form, words are no longer of much use to him. For form makes no reference to things outside the work of art. Form exists in its own right and pleases or displeases the eye for no other reason than that it is pleasant or unpleasant. One can say, "I like that picture because it is a good symbol of tenderness or a clever rendering of a pretty girl," but when one begins to say, "I like that picture because its shapes, patterns, harmonies, masses, and linear construction are . . ." one can only finish the sentence with a vague adjective— "pleasant," "well-organized," "bold." Form makes no reference to human experience: it is an end in itself. There is something so ultimate about what we are pleased to call the æsthetic emotion that it cannot be described in terms of anything but itself. One can only say feebly, "I like the colour-scheme of that picture, because it is likeable." To say, " I like it because it reminds me of moonlight on white marble," is to speak of something other than æsthetics. It is to speak of the picture as a reference to something outside the picture.

It is true that the form of a work of art can *reinforce* its power to refer to human experience, as when Forster says about the form of Thaïs, "If it were not for this hour-glass, the story, the plot and the characters would none of them exert their full force." There is a drawing by Picasso called "Zephyr," in which the basic idea of the form is one of fluttering lines contrasted with lines that just deviate from the vertical. The result is that the eye is given a sense of tremulous movement accompanied by slight instability which *reinforces* the subject-matter of the picture, though it is not in itself the subject-matter. It is even possible that in the final analysis, the æsthetic emotions are themselves deeply rooted in human experience, and that the appreciation of form in art is not altogether independent of association. Seurat worked out detailed theories of how horizontal lines were associated with peace, vertical lines with energy, and so forth. It may be that what one calls purely formal values do not, after all, exist entirely in their own right. If so, I am not a sufficiently expert psychologist to analyse their connection with human experience. In the case of the four Madonnas I can only say (without being able to give reasons) that, considered for their form alone, the Russian ikon pleases me most, with the simple yet sinuous sweep of its lop-sided pyramid, the placing of the hands, the contrast between the tight pattern of folds in the child's robe and the dark unbroken surface of the Madonna's, the combination of delicacy and strength in the lines, the queerness of the shapes (queer, again, in their own right, not merely queer in their violent distortion of human anatomy) and the relation between the mass occupied by the two figures and the plain background broken only by the hair-line of the Madonna's halo and the monogram. Next I feel drawn to the Raphael with its much greater complexity and yet much greater monotony and lower vitality. Again the basic form is a pyramid, but a more obvious, less subtle pyramid. There is a "rightness" in the choice of just where the horizontal of the water's edge cuts across the edges of the pyramid. There is a lack of those delightful contrasts between plain and patterned, between sinuous and angular, that one finds in the ikon. Everything has a calculated perfection, but the calculation behind the perfection is a shade too apparent. For example, the blocking of the horizontal water-line by the trees at either end, and the emphasis given to the two angles at the base of the pyramid by stressing the Madonna's foot on the right and St. John's foot on the left, are just a little too easy. They strike one as tricks. Simone's Madonna has none of the bigness of form of these two, though it is more refined and sensitive than either. Tiepolo's, compared with the other three, is almost formless. It is nicely placed within the four bounding lines; there is a smug kind of balance in the disposition of the masses, but it is the reflection of a commonplace vision. The artist's perpetual problem of reconciling the claims of representation and the claims of decoration has hardly been tackled in this case.

The purely decorative or formal element in painting and sculpture is therefore one which the critic and historian must always be content to take for granted. It is of the utmost importance, and yet its precise nature can never be explained. This unfortunately is bound to limit the scope and upset the balance of any book about the arts, whether it be philosophical or historical. The author, with the best will in the world, can only do justice to one half of his subject. Not only is every man's æsthetic sensitiveness different in degree from every other man's, it is also different in kind. The æsthetically insensitive man will derive little enough pleasure from the formal values of the Russian ikon, and such pleasure as he feels will be more than counteracted by his annoyance at its failure to do justice to human anatomy. But beyond that, even the æsthetically sensitive man may not be sensitive in the same direction as the creator of the Russian ikon. The ikon happens to set up in me an instant æsthetic response—a response much more intense than I have ever got from a picture by Rembrandt, though I recognize that Rembrandt is a far greater artist than the ikon painter. I regret my limitations, but I should be ill-advised to attempt to disguise or conceal them. My own hope in writing this book is not so much to set forth the facts of the story of Art as to communicate my enthusiasm about it. The dates of Michelangelo's birth and death, whose pupil he was and whom he influenced can be stated briefly and accurately by any art historian. It is not my object to do so in this book, for I can see no value in such knowledge if it is not accompanied by an estimate of what Michelangelo stood for—what contribution he made to the vision of his time. And this understanding of what a given artist stands for must of necessity be accompanied by a love (or a hatred) of what he stands for, an enthusiasm for (or against) him.

It follows, then, that no account of the arts can escape the bias of the author's own personal enthusiasms. I am not ashamed of mine. I would rather distort my theme because of the limitations of my enthusiasms than render it colourless by suppressing them.

Take, for example, the Raphael Madonna. The art historian's business is to tell you the names and dates of the artist, to state to what "school" of painting Raphael belonged, to describe the general characteristic style of that "school," and the particular characteristic style of the artist in question. Thus: "Raphael Sanzio, 1483–1520. Umbrian School. Worked in the studio of Perugino and was influenced by him in his early work. Later came under the influence of Leonardo and Michelangelo. Shared with Perugino his sweetness but not his innocence. A master of linear composition but less inventive in his colour, which is often mediocre." All that is true enough, but it leaves the reader still wondering in what respect the world would have been poorer had Raphael never lived, and what particular pleasure he will have missed if he never sees the Dresden Madonna or the Disputa. It leaves out of account the fact that Raphael was a man with a certain quality of vision, who, whenever he made a mark with brush or pencil, could not help giving that mark a Raphaelesque flavour: that whatever he did bears the imprint of his personality, that the result of that imprint in the work of art is a personal style, and that a personal style is the final index of personal vision.

What matters then, in telling the story of art, is to examine this thing called style; to find out what interplay of forces went to the making of it in any particular case. And that brings me to job No. 4 in the making of a work of art—the translation into paint of this amalgam of symbol, representation and form; an amalgam which (the reader must forgive me if I repeat myself, but it is an important point) exists only in the artist's mind's eye until the process of translation begins.

In order to get this question of "making" clear it is necessary to imagine that the artist has a complete picture in his mind's eye of what he is going to paint. We have to suppose that in painting his Madonna he has conjured up his symbols of tenderness and divinity, has also conjured up a mental image of a flesh-and-blood mother and baby, has decided how the two can be dovetailed together, and has imagined the result of this dovetailing as having certain decorative qualities which may reinforce the subject-matter but are virtually independent of it. It then only remains for him to mix his paints, take up his brushes, prepare his flat surface and transfer the mental image to it.

Unfortunately that is an over-simplification of the problem. Unfortunately words can only convey one thought at a time. I have been compelled for the sake of clearness to pretend that jobs Nos. 1, 2 and 3 are separate (though interdependent) jobs and that job No. 4—the job of painting—is a separate and subsequent process. In the same way in a technical exposition of the three-colour process of reproduction one would show separate prints of the yellow, red and blue blocks, although none of them has any real meaning except as a contribution to the final print.

Imagine the artist as a sort of chef, a man whose purpose is to achieve an amalgam of three interdependent yet conflicting ingredients and who adds to this amalgam a fourth ingredient—

his medium—and then stirs all four together into a kind of dough, which he bakes in the oven of his craftsmanship. The result is a dish in which all the ingredients play their part but which is not a mechanical mixture (as chemists say), but a chemical compound. Once the stuff is baked you cannot separate it again into its component ingredients. Nor, of course, is it necessary to do so in order to enjoy it. And yet, even though the proof of any particular pudding may be in the eating, if we are to trace the history of puddings down the ages we must have some knowledge of what ingredients were used and how they were mixed—how chef A despised eggs so that all who followed him produced eggless puddings, until that great artist, chef B, reinstated the egg, and an eggy period followed, modified later by C, whose passion for currants and raisins altered, for the time being, the attitude of mind of half a continent towards the making of puddings: how the chefs of the East based their puddings on rice and invariably served them cold, while those of the West made them of flour and liked them piping hot. What is important for us is to enjoy the pudding, not to analyse it, but at least one approach to enjoyment lies through analysis, provided it is the kind of analysis that always keeps the end in mind and is not content to think only of the means. It must be an analysis of *flavour*, the means of communicating pleasure, not of *cooking*, the method of practising a craft.

Every work of art—every picture or statue—has its own flavour—its style. An artist's style is not a thing he deliberately adopts, though it is a thing he can exploit or develop. Like a man's handwriting or the tone of his voice, it is an inevitable part of himself. It is his personality made manifest. Tell a dozen artists to draw a curved line on a piece of paper and you will get a dozen different results—different flavours of line. Some will draw boldly, others hesitatingly, some of the lines will be hard and steely, others delicate and sensitive, some will remind you of a thread of silk laid on the paper, others of a piece of bent wire. Each of those twelve lines will be an index of a different kind of man, and from the quality of the line—its style—you can deduce the man.

If a mere curved line can give so much evidence about its author, how much more complete will be the evidence of a complex work like a painting of a Madonna and Child. At every turn the artist will give himself away. He will reveal his attitude to his employer, his feelings about Madonnas, his keenness of observation, the retentiveness of his visual memory, his sense

of design, his capacity to control his brushes and his paint.
Style is the accumulated result of all this evidence. To take the
evidence supplied by a single picture or statue is no easy task.
To write the story of art is to take the evidence supplied by all
the works of art created by man since civilization began—a
manifestly impossible thing to do. Within the narrow limits
allotted to me I can hope to do no more than select a few outstanding works, typical of their creators, of their period, or of
the race to which their creators belonged, and note what seems
to me to be most important in what they reveal.

So far I have scrupulously avoided the word "beauty,"
though I have come perilously near it in discussing the æsthetic
emotion. On page 22 occurs the following sentence: "Form
exists in its own right and pleases or displeases the eye for no
other reason than that it is pleasant or unpleasant." In writing
that sentence I was uncomfortably aware of standing on the
edge of an abyss. If I had written "for no other reason than
that it is beautiful or ugly," I should have been over into the
abyss, a lost man, whose only chance of climbing out again
would be to formulate a definition of beauty. Having no such
definition, believing indeed that no definition is possible, I shall
not venture into the abyss, but merely stand on the edge and look
down into it. It is an abyss in which many a writer on æsthetics
has been lost, and I see no reason to take so dangerous and so
futile a plunge.

And yet the words "beauty" and "ugliness" are on every
man's lips and especially when art is under discussion. There
seems to be a general assumption that what the artist wishes to
produce is beauty. And tangled up with that assumption is
frequently another—seldom admitted, but one reads it between
the lines—that a picture of an ugly thing is an ugly picture,
regardless of the fact that masterpieces like Velasquez's "Las
Meninas" and Rembrandt's "Carcass of an Ox" (to take extreme
cases) are "about" subjects generally recognized as ugly. There
is a pretty general agreement about beauty and ugliness in nature.
Waterfalls, shady glens, sunsets, snow-mountains, beech trees
in spring seem beautiful to most people. Dwarfs, dustbins,
dungheaps and flayed oxen strike most people as ugly. It would
be futile to ask why. Nor has the reason why any bearing on
the present inquiry. I suspect in each case that nothing is
beautiful or ugly but thinking makes it so. A flayed ox is associated in one's thoughts with death and a dustbin with uselessness. No doubt if a vegetable marrow could express an opinion

it would become lyrical in praise of dungheaps. Faced with a flayed ox, Rembrandt *did* become lyrical, for, though to his mind it may have been a symbol of death, to his eye it presented a colour scheme of blushing pinks and translucent creams as delicate as any rose garden.

Beauty, then, to the artist, is merely the result of an attitude of mind. If the painter's visual responses are quickened by the play of light, then a dustbin can be, to him, as beautiful as a débutante. If structure and the interplay of planes excites him, then a pair of boots is, to him, more exciting than a wood carpeted with bluebells, and an old pair of boots more exciting than a new pair.

This is a commonplace of art criticism, but it does not explain the curious fact that our sense of beauty changes. Even with regard to natural objects like waterfalls and mountains it changes. Dr. Johnson and his age regarded a mountain as a rather uncouth object. "Frowning" or "horrid" were the kind of adjectives the Eighteenth Century applied to precipices. Much more does the spectator's sense of beauty shift with regard to works of art. The kind of controversy that springs up every time Mr. Epstein carves a new statue is not evidence, for it is not certain that posterity will ever regard Mr. Epstein's statues as beautiful. The chances are, however, that posterity will, for all the evidence goes to show that a man who feels intensely and expresses unhesitatingly something that has not been felt or expressed before will eventually persuade the rest of the world to share his feeling. And—this is the crux of the matter—once mankind has accepted a new type of vision and expression as valid it invariably agrees to call the work of art embodying the vision "beautiful."

One has only to draw up a list of artists who were in their day innovators and who have since been generally accepted as good artists and then to look up the contemporary criticism of their works to see the process at work. Turner's "Fighting Téméraire," Constable's "Hay Wain," Whistler's etchings of Venice, Manet's "Olympia," are obvious instances. To-day's opinion generally agrees to call them "beautiful." Their contemporaries on the whole were puzzled and hostile. "Tawdry" was the adjective applied to Turner's picture, "unnatural" to Constable's, "obscene" to Manet's. The pictures themselves remain the same. What has happened is that they have persuaded us to accept them. They have changed *us*.

The odd thing is that while the number of works we agree to

call beautiful is always increasing as this process of persuasion goes on, the reverse process rarely happens. We do not, on the whole, discover that works previously thought beautiful no longer seem to us to be so. In a few cases it has happened, as when the Bolognese eclectics, so admired by Sir Joshua Reynolds and the connoisseurs of his time, fell from favour. It happens, too, by a mysterious law which makes fashionable things look dowdy the moment they have gone out of fashion. But that is a mere temporary eclipse. Another generation goes by and what was once fashionable and later became dowdy emerges from both the artificial light and the artificial shadow. Doubtless to an Elizabethan dandy the modes of Henry VIII's day seemed deplorably unlovely. To us they are simply different, and the difference is not one that can be expressed in terms of greater or less beauty.

Beauty, then, is an almost meaningless word if one attempts to attach to it any absolute value. It is merely a convenient and ingenious piece of shorthand. "That picture of the Madonna is beautiful" is merely an extremely compressed way of saying, "In that picture the artist has succeeded in communicating to me certain of his own personal excitements about Madonnahood and about line and colour. In looking at it I begin to share those excitements. The picture has enlarged my experience. Having looked at it I shall never feel quite the same again about Madonnas or about the interplay between dark blue and gold."

Beauty in a work of art is merely an attribute we read into it the moment it begins to communicate its message. One can even watch the process, in oneself, of a work of art *becoming* beautiful as its message gradually dawns on one. I can remember my own early failure to understand the Post-Impressionists and my consequent feeling that their works were ugly, followed by a gradual comprehension and the consequent gradual birth in myself of a new sense of beauty.

The artist who is capable of being moved or excited by something—some aspect of visual experience—that has never moved or excited any artist before him is certain to be either ignored or detested until he has succeeded in persuading others to share his excitement, unless he is serving so vital a social need that his originality of vision passes unnoticed. At first a few exceptionally sensitive people will grasp the new message and welcome it. Others, slower in their response, will follow, until there is a general acceptance. At that moment the artist's work becomes (literally *becomes*) "beautiful."

It is for that reason that the very word which has attached itself most firmly to the arts, which seems indeed to provide the ultimate test of their validity, must be viewed with the utmost suspicion. "Beauty" is a word that does good service in everyday conversation. It ties together in a haphazard but useful way a host of human experiences, but in telling the story of art I shall try (doubtless not always successfully) to avoid it. It leads its users into too many pitfalls.

CHAPTER III

EAST AND WEST

ROUGHLY speaking, the story of art is the story of two unconnected groups of artists with quite different points of view. There is the Oriental group and the European group, and though this book confines itself to Western art, it will be as well, before going any further, to consider briefly the main differences between the two groups. Oriental art is rather like a complicated system of canals that run parallel with each other but sometimes intersect. Occidental art is like a river in which there is a single central current to which new tributaries are constantly being added and whose character is constantly modified by them. The study of Oriental art, therefore, involves the historian in a set of separate journeys: the study of European art is the study of a steadily evolving organism. A Chinese painting has in it an air of finality; a European painting always seems to have evolved from a set of earlier conceptions and to contain within itself the seeds of later ones.

These two groups do not, of course, cover the whole field of human art-activity. Man, in whatever part of the earth's surface, at whatever period of history and in whatever stage of civilization, has always evolved (among other kinds of language) a visual language. Negro art, Mexican and Peruvian art, to take two random examples, belong to separate branches of the language. But for the purposes of this chapter they can be left out of account. Asia and Europe have provided the bulk of the world's art, and the best of it. It is not easy to describe the difference between the two approaches to the problem of expression, but if almost any Oriental and European work of art be set side by side, one feels at once the gulf between them. A portrait or a landscape by a Chinese artist of the Sung period and say a portrait by Velasquez or a landscape by Constable seem to have been called into being by two different sets of forces working in different directions. So do a carving from an Indian temple and a statue by Donatello, or a Persian miniature and a page from Richard II's Bible of the late Fourteenth Century. To define those forces and indicate the directions in which they operate would require an exhaustive comparison between Oriental and Occidental states of mind, religions and social structures. It will be easier to point out a few obvious differences between typical works of art of the East and West.

There have been occasional instances of a link between the two, the most obvious being the Byzantine artists who managed for a time, and somewhat precariously, to keep one foot in both camps. But eventually the Italian Byzantines were occidentalized, while the Russian Byzantines were either orientalized or else proved sterile. But such links are exceptional. The two main schools have been, for the greater part of recorded history, unconnected.

Take for example the two landscapes, Figures 9 and 10. It strikes one at once that the European painter has been trying to describe a particular stretch of country seen at a particular season of the year, time of day and state of weather, and observed from a particular spot, while the Chinese painter has preferred to suggest an aspect of nature in a certain mood. The one is Constable's personal record of a particular bit of England, the other a formalized expression of man in communion with nature.

That is not to say that the Oriental painter does not observe nature as closely as the Occidental. He observes her with perhaps even more concentration, but in a different spirit. Where the European is content to translate a given scene into paint, the Oriental absorbs the whole district into his system and then gives it off again in terms of brushwork.

"But that is what you said *all* artists do," the reader may object. Certainly. But where the European artist seems to feel the need for the specific case and wishes to tie up his symbol as firmly as possible to a particular personal experience, the Oriental shuns the particular case and his symbol seems to represent the pooled experience of mankind.

The result is that Oriental art is not concerned with the nature of visual experience as is the art of the West. The work of art is not a picture of a particular thing, and therefore the laws that govern the appearance of things are of very little importance.

The discovery of the laws of perspective seemed to the Florentines a major landmark in the progress of art: perspective is largely absent from Oriental art. The Persian miniaturist who wishes to indicate that one thing is *behind* another (i.e. further away from the artist's eye than another) indicates the fact not by making the distant object smaller but by placing it higher up the picture. After all, who is the artist that his eye should determine the relative size of things? Why should he expect everyone who looks at his picture to accept *his* personal, temporary point of view? Why should the eye and not the mind be the final arbiter?

Again Oriental art is not concerned with light and shade, since light and shade are accidents that have no connection with the objects on which they fall. For the painter's purposes there are no cast shadows east of Constantinople. The result of this Oriental preoccupation with the essence rather than the appearance of the subject is to give the work of art a look which Europeans call "decorative," though decoration is not the Chinese artist's primary concern. Like Constable, the Chinese landscapist is concerned with truth, but truth of a different kind. Constable takes the utmost pains to be faithful to what his eye sees: the Eastern artist to what his mind knows.

The effect of this difference of outlook between the two is to make the one static and the other evolutionary—or as I have already said, to make one resemble a system of parallel canals, the other a river. For the Eastern, "development" or "progress" in the art of painting can hardly be said to exist. He is not engaged, as the European is, in a struggle with the image on his retina. One half of the story of European painting is concerned with the gradual discovery of what things "look like." Rembrandt knew far more than Giotto about the "look" of things, and most art students of to-day know as much as Rembrandt. That does not make Rembrandt a greater artist than Giotto nor does it make the art student the equal of Rembrandt, but it alters the equipment they bring to the job of painting, and therefore it alters their style. But to the Oriental artist style is not a thing that develops with time. It is a thing that can and must be varied according to the requirements of the subject. A European painting can usually be dated to within a couple of decades. It is difficult to place an Oriental painting to within a century.

In looking at so static an art one has no sense of a battle against odds. The Oriental mind's eye does not snatch greedily at what the physical eye offers it. It digests it calmly and a curious refinement and sensitiveness of line, and especially of spacing, result, which make almost any European painting look rough and clumsy by comparison. Even the most controlled and ascetic of European painters—even a Mantegna or an Ingres —seems uncouth by contrast.

But the most noticeable difference between the two approaches to painting is that whereas the European has always insisted on making every square inch of his picture a reference to the artist's visual experience, the Oriental feels no such need. An unbroken area of paint above a European landscape is a *representation* of a cloudless sky. A corresponding unbroken area in an Oriental landscape simply means that the Oriental artist did not choose to make any statement whatever about the sky. It is not a representation of a cloudless sky but a portion of the painting in which the artist had not given any visual information at all. It is a resting space for the eye—like a pause in music.

A comparison between the Sung artist's picture of ladies preparing silk and Courbet's of girls preparing for a wedding on figures 7 and 8 (the contrast between the two subjects is in itself an index of the difference between a race of men that contemplates a generalized activity and one that observes a particular incident) shows exactly what I mean. The groups—remarkably similar in the "story" they tell—of women holding a length of cloth, are seen in utterly different ways. Courbet's women are in a room, standing on the floor, surrounded by air. Unimportant though their environment may be in itself, Courbet has no alternative but to describe it. Not so the Chinese artist. He paints his women and the stretch of cloth they hold, and beyond that he has no obligation. The blank space behind them does not mean that they are floating in mid air or that they have no surroundings or environment. It is not a painter's description of a vacuum but an artist's provision of a resting place for the spectator's eye and mind.

Instances could be piled up indefinitely of how the difference between the two points of view gives the two families of art a difference of direction. Freed from the obligations imposed on the Western artist by his gross visual appetites and his nagging visual curiosity, the Eastern artist is not distracted by the tug of war between his æsthetic duty and his descriptive duty that has been described in an earlier chapter. A green robe is to him a green robe, not a surface whose colour is modified by the impact of light on one side and the absence of it on the other. He can therefore rejoice to his heart's content in its greenness. He does not have to wonder, as Leonardo did, whether green in shadow is best represented by the addition of black to the basic green or by hinting at its complementary colour red—a problem that was not solved until the Impressionist tackled it in the Nineteenth Century. Unhampered by an urge to explore the nature of light (which is a branch of optical science) the Oriental is free to explore far more thoroughly than the European the possibilities of colour (which is a branch of æsthetics).

In sculpture where, for obvious reasons, there is a less violent line of cleavage between the thing-in-itself and the thing-as-it-appears-to-the-eye-of-the-artist, the difference between East and West is not quite so startling, but it is never in any doubt. Behind every Western carving of a human figure is the implication of a portrait; behind every Oriental statue is the implication of a mood. The idea of serenity has never been quite so intensely caught and held by any European sculptor as it has by countless of the cross-legged Buddhas of Ceylon. Nor has the idea of sinuous movement as expressed in Indian carvings of dancers ever been equalled in the West.

From all this the reader may gather that I consider Oriental art to be somehow on a higher plane than European, and that consequently I find it somehow more admirable. What I have said might certainly give that impression. And yet the reader would be wrong. The bulk of Oriental art by its very calmness and detachment leaves me cold. It is too exquisite, too inhuman. The Chinese ladies who hold out that lovely length of silk with its faintly sagging curve, cutting across its horizontal line with their own vertical lines, are too much like a sample of Chinese calligraphy. Human beings in Chinese art are no longer specimens of *homo sapiens*. They are examples of *homo aestheticus*. In their rarefied presence I begin to long for Courbet's giggling, sweating wenches. Chinese brushwork may be compact of vital rhythms, but I prefer Titian's (relatively) clumsy piling on of paint and his (by comparison) bucolic attempts to make it satisfy his rough-and-tumble needs. To the European, laughter and sweat are a necessary part of art as well as of life. I have seen Chinese paintings made of lines as subtle as a silken thread blown on to the paper, and tones as elusive as the smoke of a cigarette. And yet—and yet I cannot be content with an art that leaves my more material appetites unsatisfied. I like to think of the artist as in some way part of his subject: that Titian, painting his "Bacchus and Ariadne," was an unofficial member of Bacchus's attendant crew of satyrs, and that half the picture's vitality springs from this close contact with life. No Chinese artist would permit such a sense of contact. He holds himself aloof, and *his* picture's vitality must spring from a set of vital rhythms set up in his mind and communicated by his fingers to the points of his brush.

So much for 'the fundamental difference between the Oriental point of view with its parallel schools and its contemplative habit of mind, and the Occidental with its evolutionary system in which contemplation is replaced by a visual curiosity that is always leading the artist into new discoveries, each of which becomes embedded in the central tradition, enlarging it, modifying it and deflecting it, but never allowing it to settle down into a rigid system.

CHAPTER IV

THE DEVELOPMENT OF EUROPEAN ART

THE nature of European art makes it necessary to inquire not only into its general characteristics but also into the circumstances of its birth, childhood, and advance to maturity. It must be treated as an organism capable of all these developments and also liable to periods of debility and (the implications of the analogy must be faced) possibly a period of senility and decay.

Its birth is vague enough. The art of Egypt, static and self-contained for centuries in the Nile Valley, had none of the restless curiosity, the search for new worlds to conquer, that characterize European art. But it was from Egypt that the seeds blew across to the Eastern Mediterranean and took root among the Aegean Islands. The first signs of growth became apparent in Mycenæ and Crete. After the hieratic perfection of Egypt the art of the Cretans and Mycenæans is amateurish, but it is full of vigour and unlike Egyptian art it refuses to rely on a set of conventions. Greece caught this vigorous spirit and nourished it with that type of intellectual curiosity that gave the whole of Greek culture its solid foundation and permitted its subsequent growth to be more capable of refinement than anything that had come before it. The rigidity of the early statues of Greek athletes gradually relaxed into dignity, then into grace and finally into prettiness. The same process can be traced in the only paintings that have survived, those on the vases. Greece had to all intents and

purposes only one message to communicate in her visual arts—
the beauty of the human body. For all her intellectual curiosity
—and perhaps because of it—she had no conception of the
human soul nor did she attempt to express anything but her
admiration of the physical in her art.

Rome, heavier, emptier, less creative, could neither add anything to what the Greeks had said nor had she any desire to break
away from it. Nothing new could be said in the Greek idiom. It
seemed for a moment as if the original source—the pagan source
—from which the stream of European art was to spring, had
dried up.

Meanwhile another and exactly contradictory motive force was
gathering momentum further East. Greek paganism adored the
body. Christianity equally whole-heartedly adored the soul.

The origin of the Byzantine style presents a problem which has
not yet been seriously faced, still less solved. What makes it
important is that it marks the beginning of a complete cycle in art
history, a double swing of the pendulum, which has perhaps just
ended. It is easy enough to think of European art as progressing
from "primitive" to "mature," from decorative and symbolic to
naturalistic and descriptive. The progression seems a natural one,
but that I think is only because the pendulum constantly swings
backwards and forwards between the two, and we in the Twentieth
Century happen to have just come to the end of a long swing
towards the descriptive and away from the symbolic. But at the
fall of the Roman Empire, when a materialistic religion was
giving way to a spiritual one, the exact reverse was taking place.
The Seventh and Sixth Centuries B.C. produced stark archaic
figures; the Fifth and Fourth produced the softened and rounded
forms of the golden age of Greece. That seems a natural progression and one would have thought that to whatever extent subject-
matter might change, the honeyed perfection of the period from
Pericles to Augustus could never give way to a more primitive
style. And yet we find the Sixth Century A.D. producing a style as
stiff (though not as stark) as that of early Greece. This backward
pendulum-swing embraces the whole of the Byzantine period,
which was certainly not an age of ignorance or of incompetence.
Craftsmanship in the arts was certainly at a high level, and the
Christian Church took the utmost pains to control its direction
and turn it into an effective propagandist machine. It is only we,
nourished as we have been on a naturalistic tradition, who regard
the swing away from descriptive naturalism as a swing *backwards*.
Doubtless the devotees of the decaying Græco-Roman paganism

were also shocked at the gradual rise of the new style spreading westwards from Byzantium, but that did not prevent it spreading. The pendulum swung until Giotto, with one of those magnificent single-handed gestures that make ordinary mortals seem weak and timid, stopped it dead and started it swinging back through the cycle with which we are now familiar, Giotto, Masaccio, Raphael, Titian, Rembrandt, Monet, Cézanne. Draw a line through those seven names and you get a curve which is the graph of the last full forward swing of the pendulum; the centre of that curve is marked by the Renaissance, and the end of it, if my reading of the evolution of Western art is correct, by the death of Cézanne. The pendulum has now begun to swing back again, but it has not yet swung far enough to justify any attempts at detailed prophecy about the sort of curve it will take.

Any history of art written for the consumption of twentieth-century Europeans must necessarily regard the Giotto-Cézanne period (say 1300–1900) as the most important section of art history and must devote far more space to those six centuries than to any other period—the (approximately) hundred centuries of Palæolithic art, the eighty centuries or so of Neolithic art, the thirty centuries of Egyptian, the twelve centuries of the Cretan-Roman cycle, or the eleven centuries of Early Christian art. Those six centuries mark the gradual solution of one problem after another in the conquest of appearances. The solution of those problems had nothing whatever to do with the greatness of the artists involved, nor with the potency with which they communicated their message. It revolutionized the artist's means but it brought him no nearer to his end. Giotto, unaware of one half of the problems yet to be solved, is still a giant, immeasurably more potent than the host of later artists who could solve them with the greatest ease. What still matters is the *intensity* of the artist's vision, not its scope. Nevertheless, the development of period-vision is a fascinating thing to follow, and the object of the high-speed journey undertaken in this chapter is to establish a rough outline of its direction, leaving the assessment of genius for later enquiry.

Giotto stopped the pendulum by virtue of his humanity and his sense of drama. The Byzantines, hieratic, aristocratic, conservative, had created an aloof world in which the human body, so devotedly worshipped by the Greeks, had no place. Giotto gave his figures a physique and brought them back to earth; he took them out of the vague indeterminate space in which they had existed for so long and set them in definite places on the earth's surface, set them among rocks or in meadows or houses. They have structure, they breathe. They are the expression in art of the democratic conception of St. Francis. Both Giotto and St. Francis have much in common with the Salvation Army of to-day. All three base their creed on human nature rather than inhuman dogma. St. Francis turned doctrine into parable, Giotto turned it into narrative. The immense twist he gave to the general direction of art was the result of his preoccupation with the story of Christianity rather than its dogma.

After Giotto the current of the stream slackened a little, but Masaccio a century later carried the Giottesque humanity a stage further. The spirit of Greece, with its acceptance of the human body, was latent in the Florentine primitives. It only needed the rediscovery of Greek literature and the digging up of a few Græco-Roman statues to bring out its full flavour. But harnessed as art was to Christian teaching, Florence could never produce an art based on physique alone. Just as Byzantium had taken the Græco-Roman idiom and mysticized it, so Florence took the Byzantine spirit and materialized it. Meanwhile Siena, no more than thirty miles away, had already taken the Byzantine spirit and instead of materializing it had refined it, civilized it, made it elegant and wistful. If Florence took the Byzantine world and pulled it forcibly down to earth, the Sienese lifted the earth, with its pots and pans and houses and gardens and beasts and birds, gently up into the rarefied Byzantine heaven. The method was less robust. Siena provided a delicious little tributary to the stream, but not an important one.

The Renaissance took firmer root in Florence. The harness of Christianity, hitherto universal, proved just a little too irksome for an adventurous set of men who had rediscovered the pagan world. The Madonna, they realized, was not the whole of womanhood, nor Jesus the whole of manhood. Venus and Apollo must be brought in to take their places by their sides. Again one sees the pendulum swinging back over the same ground. In the early Christian mosaics Jesus had been visualised as a kindly, beardless, rustic Apollo. In the early Renaissance pictures Venus reappears with many of the outward characteristics of the Madonna. Botticelli and Signorelli alternated between the claims of Christianity and Paganism. Michelangelo combined them and intensified their vigour. In him "physique" reaches its climax, and, as every climax must be followed by an anti-climax, the Florentine High Renaissance ecstasy began, after him, to settle down into something calmer and less vital. But Michelangelo was not in the centre of the Florentine stream. Its central figure was Raphael, who perfected the science of picture making in the same way that an engineer might perfect the science of bridge-making. If Masaccio had developed the painter's sense of structure, Raphael developed the painter's sense of balance. With him a picture is a thing in which harmony—the relation of the parts to the whole—is the prime objective.

Meanwhile in the Venetian plain another tributary, bigger than the Sienese tributary, began to make its way towards the main stream. Oddly enough it started in a direction that gave no hint of what was to be its later course. Mantegna, the most ardent "classicist" of them all, was positively fanatical in his steely austerity of line, and he bequeathed this austerity to Giovanni Bellini, his brother-in-law. But there was something in Bellini that could not be content with austerity. As his art gathered momentum he gradually shed his austerity and adopted a light-laden sensuousness that was new in European art. With light came colour—not the hard Florentine colour that belongs only to *objects*, but the glowing colour that belongs to *light*. Bellini turned the Mantegna tributary round. As it progressed away from intellectual austerity in the direction of glowing sensuous-ness it became more rapid, and in less than ten years from Bellini's first essays in the new manner, the Venetian school was in full spate, rich, joyful, exuberant. Florentine art always suggests a spring morning: Venetian a summer afternoon. The languor of a Venus by Titian (see Figure 19) is very different from the wistful-ness of a Venus by Botticelli. Raphael and Michelangelo mark the climax in Florence, Titian and Tintoretto in Venice. Again came the anti-climax, again the slackening of the stream, but not such a sudden slackening as in Florence. The two streams joined, became sluggish. Both Florence and Venice had drawn their vitality from excitement at their own visual discoveries—in the one case the discovery of structure, with it attendant emphasis on line, in the other the discovery of colour with its attendant emphasis on surface. To unite the two discoveries was an artistic problem but it was not in itself a discovery. The problem had its roots in art, not in life, and therefore it was moribund, for though art can always build on art, it cannot be vitalized unless it also draws its inspiration from life. "Art built on art" is as good a definition of the disease known as eclecticism cism as one needs. Italian art died of eclecticism.

The Renaissance radiated from Italy to all parts of Europe, but the rest of Europe had not Italy's splendid acceptance of new discoveries, nor her power to graft a pagan physique on to a medieval mysticism. In Germany, steeped in an uncouth mysticism, the Renaissance took strange forms. The intellectual curiosity which was one half of it took firm hold, but not the grace and leisureliness that was the other half. Somehow the Renaissance forms in Germany never concealed her medieval love of the grotesque and the macabre. In England the Renaissance came late, and it came as a manufactured import rather than as raw material for a nation to turn to her own uses. In architecture Wren did produce his own personal version of it, but in painting and sculpture it arrived fully grown, introduced through the medium of foreign artists, Holbein, Rubens, Van Dyck and Lely. England never knew the thrilling early stages of it as Italy did, with new worlds unfolding themselves at every turn. When France adopted it it had already settled down into a comfortable, middle-aged respectability in Rome, where the French painters Poussin and Claude took it as they found it, but gave it the stimulus of their own nervous energy. We must visualize the dancing rapids of art in Italy in the Fifteenth and Sixteenth Centuries broadening out into a placid stream and covering most of Europe in the Seenteenth.

But there were still plenty of aspects of the visual world to conquer, and the Seventeenth Century produced men who conquered them brilliantly. It was in the Seventeenth Century that two more tributaries flowed into the stream, one from Holland in the North, the other from Spain in the South-west. Dutch artists, with their genius for domesticity, succeeded during the brief period when Dutch art was at its height, in presenting a complete portrait of Protestant middle-class Holland.

Spain, aristocratic and fervently Catholic, was not nearly as prolific as Holland, but her contribution to European painting was more in the central tradition than that of Holland. It had the Italian nobility of mood and breadth of structure. El Greco, that strange creature whose personal eccentricities of style were so insistent that he can hardly be said to belong to the general pattern of European development, did at least make Spain conscious of what was happening further East. Coming straight from Venice and grasping with uncanny insight the subtle difference between Titian, the last of the Classic painters, and Tintoretto, the first of the Baroque painters, he prepared the ground in Spain for the new Baroque spirit. El Greco was abnormal: he was too individual to found a national school of painting. It was the magnificently normal Velasquez who made the seventeenth-century Spanish tributary important, just as it was Rembrandt who gathered together and intensified all that Dutch art stood for in the Seventeenth Century. The contribution of both of them towards solving the problems of representation was the same. Both had a mental grasp of the visible world which showed how incomplete had been the visual equipment of all previous painters.

This question of "grasp" is not an easy one to explain. It consists largely in the painter's power to ignore the separateness of objects, and this power is bound up with the whole conception of "Baroque" art.

The "classic" vision of the Sixteenth Century consisted of an intense realization of each object—its structure, shape and pattern, and of a power to build up a satisfying static whole out of the interdependence of the parts. There is in the Madonna by Raphael (Figure 5) an extraordinary feeling for the generalized character of each concept—the concepts "arm," "foot," "neck" and so on, all of which added together form the larger concept "woman" and the still larger concept "group of figures" and the still larger concept "group of figures" in a landscape." The Sixteenth Century at its best could, out of a set of perfect parts, build up a perfect whole. Earlier stages of art found this difficult. The painter could grasp the smaller concepts, but failed to establish the relations between them. An extreme instance of such failure is seen in Egyptian reliefs where the concept "head" is represented by the typical view—the profile view—into which is fitted the typical view—the front view—of the eye. Both head and eye are correctly seen in themselves, but not in relation to one another. In Egyptian art the whole human body it built up on this system, with a front view of the shoulders leading into a side view of the legs and an unconvincing mixture of the two in the region of the waist. The power of the mind's eye to grasp larger and larger units of form is acquired only after a struggle and only in later stages of development. The fifteenth-century Italian painter's command of the human figure had been acquired by an intense interest in and study of the human figure, but the power to relate figures to each other was a later development. In Andrea del Castagno's version of the "Last Supper" each of the thirteen figures is a separately solved problem. In Leonardo's the figures are tied together in compact groups of three, and each group is linked up with the next by a carefully designed connecting gesture (see

Figures 17 and 18). It is a masterly essay in classic composition and any sixteenth-century artist might forgivably have been convinced that the last word had been said in picture-construction.

But the last word had by no means been said. The mind's eye that could merge the concept "man" in the larger concept "group of men" was as yet incapable of grasping the concept "man-in-his-environment." Leonardo's sense of the relationship between his thirteen figures and the room in which they sit is almost as elementary as the Egyptian sculptor's sense of the relationship between a human eye and a human head. It was a discovery of the Seventeenth Century (with Rembrandt as its central figure), that the whole complex texture of visible form could be taken in with one comprehensive sweep of the mind's eye. The artist's vision was no longer ruled by concepts. Rembrandt was no longer conscious of painting a set of definable and therefore separable objects. His eye could pass from a figure to the floor under its feet and the wall behind it and the cloud seen through the window in the wall without being conscious of passing from one *thing* to another. The whole texture of his picture is one.

Again, a hundred scraps of evidence can be cited to show how this new type of mind's eye produced a new kind of picture. Leonardo's way of looking at life was essentially the same as the Egyptian sculptor's way of looking at a man. He selected the typical view—the front view, the audience's view of a stage. Leonardo's thirteen men are seated at a table that lies exactly at right-angles to the spectator's line of vision. Like scenery on the stage every plane in his picture is parallel to this table line. And, as in the theatre, one has a sneaking sense that if one went round into the wings the whole thing would lose its apparent solidity. But with the Seventeenth Century, the breakaway from the method of working by separate concepts also meant a breakaway from frontality. The artist can now paint his picture from any angle. In Tintoretto's "Last Supper," in the church of San Giorgio, Venice, the table is in steep diagonal perspective. And with the breakaway from frontality comes a breakaway from symmetry. Almost every sixteenth-century picture and almost no seventeenth-century picture has a centre line.

Again, the abandonment of the classic system of using parts in order to build up a whole introduces a larger set of rhythms, which leap to the eye in all the arts but are perhaps most noticeable in architecture. The notion of a building as a structure made up like a bookcase by adding storey to storey gives way to a system in which every effort is made to disguise the separate storeys by such devices as running great columns or pilasters from top to bottom of the façade. Sometimes, not content with the concept "building," the architect even linked up his structure with the ground on which it stood by a system of terraces or a crowd of statues running forward from it but architecturally related to it.

The earlier faith in line, the system of describing objects by insisting on their contour, has now given place to a faith in surface and an even greater faith in light. For if the artist can take in the whole complex texture of nature at one eyeful, dividing lines between objects cease to have a meaning. If there is no longer an essential differentiation to be made between a man and the shadow he casts on the wall behind him, why draw a line between them? If the two merge in nature, then let them merge on the canvas.

The earlier faith in the picture as a tableau that recedes from the eye in a set of parallel planes has given place to a type of vision in which receding planes are lost in a continuous receding movement. One can think of a sixteenth-century picture as an elevation. To understand a seventeenth-century picture one must also think of its ground plan.

All this, and a good deal more, is summed up in the word "Baroque," a word which is too commonly used to mean merely "rhetorical." Rhetoric certainly was typical of the Seventeenth Century, for it was a pompous, worldly age and rhetoric flourished in it. But rhetoric is a mere by-product of it. Velasquez was no rhetorician and certainly nothing could be less rhetorical than the exquisite restraint of Vermeer of Delft. Any formula that will describe the basic spirit of the Seventeenth Century must be one that includes the Vermeers and Watteaus as well as the Rubenses and the Berninis. "Baroque" Art in its deeper sense finally rejects the idea that a work of art is a sum of parts. The unbroken rhythm that runs through a baroque painting or statue comes into being because there is nothing in the artist's mind— no splitting up of life into mankind and its background—to break the rhythm. A sixteenth-century drawing is always a drawing of an isolated object—a horse, an angel or a fold of drapery: but almost any seventeenth-century drawing, even the merest scribble, places the object in its surroundings.

Further progress in this direction being manifestly impossible, the Eighteenth Century was content to reflect in its arts its own social background. Pedestrian, protestant Holland had said all she had to say by the end of the Seventeenth Century. Spain still had one major artist to come—Goya. Italy and Germany had no further contributions to make to the main European tradition. The late Seventeenth Century saw the artistic centre of gravity shift to Paris where it has remained till the present day.

Artistically the Eighteenth Century was a comparatively uncreative period. It was the age of reason. Or rather it alternated between reasonableness and playfulness neither of which is creative as religion is creative. Reason can produce refinement and playfulness decoration. And with the exception of Watteau no typical eighteenth-century artist produced anything more than good decoration or a refinement on the achievement of previous artists. Poussin refined on the Venetians, Boucher made a decorative background for Louis XV and the Pompadour. What the Eighteenth and Nineteenth Centuries expressed was not a way of looking at nature, a habit of sight, but a way of living, a habit of mind. And the French habit of mind has always been logical and clear-cut, the moods reflected in painting and sculpture since the beginning of the Eighteenth Century were also clear-cut. First the playful Rococo of Louis XVI, then the cold pseudo-noble classicism of the Empire, then the romantic Byronic mood of the early Nineteenth Century, then the school that called itself "realist." These were not so much styles as fashions. They were reflections of political or social conceptions rather than of an attitude to the visual world. True, they produced new and interesting phases in painting. Classicism produced David and Ingres, Romanticism Delacroix and Géricault, Realism was founded by Courbet, but none of these movements shed any new light on the visible world as the Classic and the Baroque movements had done. They were ways of thinking and feeling, not ways of seeing or visualizing.

It was not till Impressionism turned its attention to the nature of light and especially to the colour of shadow that painters evolved a new way of seeing. The meaning of Impressionism will be discussed in a later chapter. It was not a very important set of discoveries that the Impressionists made, but it had a remarkable effect on the appearance of pictures. I have already tried to explain how the artist's search for a new aspect of truth produces in the long run a new type of what we are pleased to call beauty. Impressionism furnishes a remarkably clear instance of the process. The Impressionists were concerned almost to the exclusion of everything else in representing what light and shadow really *looked* like. To that they were willing to sacrifice, if necessary, most of the things that previous ages had held dear—form, structure, balance, even humanity. But in the pursuit of this almost exclusively scientific end they evolved a new set of colour schemes and tonalities. The final effect of Impressionism was to clean up the painter's palette, to banish browns and blacks, to bring back the primary and secondary colours and to lighten the whole tone of painting. It is the Impressionists who have taught us to think of the "old masters" as dark and mellow. They revolutionized the European colour-sense. In their pursuit of visual truth they were the last of their kind; their effort was as it were a death rattle of the cycle of realism that had begun with Giotto and ended with Cézanne. But the particular truth they found—truth of colour—was in perfect accord with the new, non-realistic phase that began after Cézanne.

That phase is in its infancy. Cézanne was a beginning and an end. He was in one sense the last of the Impressionists because he adopted their colour-sense and grafted his own discoveries on to it. In another he was, as he called himself, "the primitive" of a new way of painting. That new way is not yet half a century old. At present Picasso seems to be its central figure, but it is too early to say whether Picasso is an isolated phenomenon or is crystallizing the new set of traditions.

But wherever the new traditions may be heading for, European art since Cézanne has certainly entered on a new phase—the phase we have agreed to call "modern"; and with its inauguration the artist's six-century-long attempt to capture the truth of appearances with his brush, as an entomologist pursues a butterfly, has come to an end. Whatever the present phase is after, it is not after *that* kind of truth.

CHAPTER V

THE STONE AGE

THE earliest known examples of representational painting are almost exactly what one would expect them not to be. If the Abbé Breuil's careful copies of the painted animals that were discovered in a cave at Altamira in Spain sixty years ago were to be mounted and framed and hung in a mixed exhibition of contemporary art they would probably pass unnoticed. Possibly some critic might write "Among the drawings, Mr. X's vigorous 'Female Bison Leaping' shows keen powers of observation." But the critic would certainly not suspect that these drawings that seem so much at home in the Twentieth Century A.D. were accurate copies from paintings made in about the Two Hundredth Century B.C.

For many years after their discovery the authenticity of these paintings was suspected by critics and archaeologists alike. But in 1895, similar drawings were discovered in the caves of La Mouthe, and to-day more than fifty caves are known to contain drawings from the same period. How long ago they were done is not known to within a score of centuries; the probable limits of the Palæolithic period which produced them are between ten and thirty thousand years ago. The best of them are those first discovered at Altamira, painted in a limited range of colour, black and red predominating.

Our imaginary critic who had airily dismissed these drawings with his stock adjective "vigorous" and his stock phrase "keen powers of observation," making perhaps a mental note to look out for Mr. X's promising work in other mixed exhibitions, would certainly change his tune on being told that the artist lived before writing, before cloth and pottery, perhaps before cooking had been invented. Certainly if the artist could speak at all, his command of spoken language must have been more primitive than his command of graphic language.

Even so, why *should* the critic change his tune? After all, whoever made these drawings, and whenever he lived, the drawings would still be the same. Yes, they would *be* the same, but would they *mean* the same? I think not. If Egyptologists were to discover near Cairo a building rather like St. Paul's Cathedral which could be proved to belong to the Fifth Dynasty, if in an early manuscript of Plato's Republic there suddenly occurred a sentence in pure English, if among the thirteenth-century windows of Chartres Cathedral one, hitherto unnoticed, were found to represent St. Peter using a typewriter, all one's theories would have to be revised. It would be necessary to show that the resemblance between St. Peter's thirteenth-century typewriter and a modern typewriter was a pure coincidence, like the resemblance between a chessboard and a crossword puzzle. The two things look the same but they were produced for different reasons; functionally they have no connection.

Or, to put the problem another way round, a drawing of a bison is interesting for two reasons, firstly because it tells us something about bisons, secondly because it tells us something about the man who drew the bison. A prehistoric drawing of a bison might give very much the same kind of information about bisons as a drawing by a contemporary art-student, but they would give us quite different information about the two artists if we were wise enough to interpret them correctly. Unfortunately we are not wise enough. Show me a drawing by Mr. Jones of the Slade School and I will tell you something about Mr. Jones, but about Mr. X of Altamira I can tell you very little on the evidence of his drawings. He is altogether too remote. He does not fit into the usual theory of art development, the theory that primitive man is content with a symbol, a mere diagram of his mind-image, and that as he emerges from primitiveness the diagram becomes more realistic and less decorative. My four Madonna-and-Child paintings bear out such a theory admirably, but not the bison. It is emphatically not a diagram of a mind-image. It is a descriptive record of a momentary pose observed with the swiftness of a snapshot. Until the late Nineteenth Century, when, influenced by the camera, artists began to specialize in capturing the swift momentary gesture, only a few exceptional draughtsmen had been capable of making this kind of drawing. How Palæolithic man managed to do it is a mystery. It seems almost as though civilization had somehow robbed man of his power of seeing: as though the later activities of thinking and feeling had deadened his sight so that only after a struggle lasting many centuries could civilized man see with the same penetrating eye as uncivilized man. Roger Fry has put forward an ingenious theory that with the development of language man began to see things in terms of concepts and that the use of words like "eye," "neck" and "leg" tended to concentrate his intellectual attention on each separate portion of the object seen and prevented him taking the whole thing at a glance. The theory may be correct, but it can only be speculative. To imagine a creature with the unthinking eye of an animal but with the creative urge of a man is too difficult. What is certain is that though in these drawings completely uncivilized man and hyper-civilized man have arrived at precisely the same goal, their way of reaching it must be different since their starting points are different.

Equally obscure is the reason why these Palæolithic paintings were made at all. The notion that Palæolithic man could have done them for the same reason that would prompt an art student of to-day—for the fun of doing them or for personal profit—seems inconceivable. And yet our only reason for refusing to believe that Palæolithic man would make drawings for fun is that contemporary savages usually make their drawings and carvings

for religious, superstitious or magical ends. Naturally Palæolithic man's interest in bisons cannot have been purely æsthetic.
The bison was his enemy and his dinner. Therefore he wanted to
have power over bisons: therefore he drew bisons in the same
spirit in which waxen images of a man's enemy were made in
order to give him power over his enemy. Again the theory is
plausible but purely speculative. If it is correct one would have
thought that Palæolithic man would have been content with the
crudest symbols instead of going to the trouble of making these
extraordinarily vivid essays in realism.

What is just as remarkable and just as unexpected is that
Palæolithic drawing is almost aggressively non-decorative. In
the art of savage tribes and of children there is almost always
a feeling for spacing, balance and organization, but in most of the
more ambitious paintings, notably the complex hunting scenes at
Cogul and Almeria in Spain, the confusion, the complete
absence of organization is quite painful. Deer, cattle, men and
women sprawl in confusion across the wall on which they were
painted. Evidently the faculty of organizing which involves a
certain amount of thinking was beyond the scope of these artists,
though mere seeing was well within their power. And evidently
they had evolved a visual language to record what they saw long
before they evolved a spoken language to record their thought.

Palæolithic man also carved in ivory and modelled in clay, and
here again he showed considerable power to create realistic
single images and unexpected feebleness in relating one form to
another.

Centuries later the New Stone Age that followed the Old
Stone Age left behind very little representational art. Neolithic
man was an architect, not an artist. The building of Stone-
henge is a very different kind of achievement from the drawing of
bisons and one that shows fairly clearly the direction in which
primitive man was evolving. Survivals of representational
Neolithic art are rare, and the few specimens we have—like the
little decorated human figures found in Rumania—are covered
with stripes and spirals as though to represent some elaborate
system of tattooing. The Neolithic artists were evidently more
interested in pattern than in shape. In the history of the representative arts their surviving achievements are hardly worth
recording.

CHAPTER VI

EGYPT AND MESOPOTAMIA

FOR purposes of convenience (and what historian can resist the insidious temptation of convenience?) I have divided the art of civilized man into two families, that of the West spurred on by visual curiosity, and that of the East governed by contemplation. It would make the history of art a tidier, more orderly affair if one could attach the art of Egypt and Mesopotamia to either family, but neither curiosity nor contemplation provide their motive force. Æsthetically they belong to neither group. Geographically and culturally they belong to the West if only because when the art of Egypt was decaying the artists of the Eastern Mediterranean were taking hints from its craftsmanship and copying its mannerisms. But their spirit was utterly different. The family likeness is only skin deep.

In an earlier chapter I insisted that healthy art is always harnessed to a set of social needs. That is truer of Egyptian art than of any other. The Egyptian artist was as much a servant of the Egyptian State-religion machine as the modern poster artist is of the modern commerce machine. That is even an understatement. For the modern poster artist is at liberty to invent symbols to express the desirability of the product advertised. (It is a sad comment on the poverty of his inventiveness that he can usually only think of one symbol—a pretty girl.) The Egyptian artist had not even this liberty. The symbols he used were dictated by the king and the priest. Egyptian state and religion were indivisible and the artist served them faithfully and prolifically for over thirty centuries.

For thirty centuries the Egyptian conception of both state and religion remained pretty much the same. Consequently for the same astonishing period Egyptian art hardly changed its character. It was rather like an impressive and trusted family butler who knows his place and keeps to it with a perfect but highly artificial code of manners. Its duties remained unchanged: its way of carrying out its duties hardly varied: therefore its style was incapable of real development.

The comparison between Egyptian art and a butler would be a good one if it were not that we are rather fond of butlers.

Beneath the impassive façade of the perfect butler we feel that there lurks a heart of gold. We know that down in the servants' hall he unbends, and that if ever his master is in serious trouble the façade will vanish and reveal the human being behind it. But the polished and frightening perfection of Egyptian art is not a façade. It is solid. Instead of the butler's "Certainly, my lord. I hope I shall give satisfaction," in Egyptian art there is an implied "It shall be done." It is the robot's response. Egyptian sculpture (and to a less extent Egyptian paint) is cold. It bears the same sort of relation to humanity that a man's last will and testament does to his deathbed mood.

The land of Egypt and its backbone, the Nile, were as indissoluble as Egyptian state and religion—and as self-contained. To the south was the source of the river, and beyond that were barbarians, but the Egyptians were not a nation of soldiers, so the barbarians were left in peace. To the north was the Nile's delta, and beyond that the sea, but the Egyptians were not sailors, so the sea was left uncharted and unexplored. Fresh ideas infiltrated with difficulty at either end. Egyptian civilization just rolled on, like the Nile itself, for century after century, teeming with life like an ant-hill, trusting to the momentum of its own rhythm, extraordinarily efficient but completely conservative.

To be sure, Egyptologists will divide your Egyptian history for you into three periods, with a prehistoric period at the beginning, two intermediate periods between them, and a period of decay tacked on at the end. And art-historians, grossly exaggerating the importance of detail as art-historians always do, will tell you how the Egyptian style changed with those periods, now vigorous, now refined, now pompous, now trivial. That is true. Even the family butler has his moods. Even the robot is not quite consistent. But to the average European Egyptian art has one of the most unchanging flavours in the whole history of art. There is less difference between a seated statue of King Kephren, carved in 2800 B.C., and one of King Rameses II done fifteen centuries later than there is between a doge's portrait by Giovanni Bellini and one painted by Titian fifteen years later. It is therefore more important in this condensed sketch to think of Egyptian art as a whole than to split critical hairs about the difference between the styles of the Old Kingdom, the Middle Kingdom and the New Kingdom.

The keynote of Egyptian religion was a mystical materialism. That is not a contradiction in terms. The Egyptian belief in a life inhering in the corpse after death is a mystical one. But the

Egyptian conception of that life as an exact replica of life on this earth as he knew it is a materialistic one. Egyptian art centres round the tomb. (The pyramid is only one, the most impregnable, form of tomb.) It is the art of the cemetery into which the idea of decay was never allowed to enter. Death is an unfortunate occurrence that must be recognized but never allowed to break the continuity. When the machine runs down a hundred agents must see to it that the wheels do not cease to revolve. And of those agents the most important was the artist.

In the later stages of Egyptian civilization (from the Eighteenth Dynasty onwards: say from 1500 B.C. to about 500 B.C.) not only tombs, but temples were furnished by the artist; but the ultimate object of both was the same. The tombs served the practical purpose of preserving the dead, together with everything from a saucepan to a musical instrument that he might need in his life-after-death: the temples had the more mystical one of keeping him on good terms with the gods who provided the facilities for this continued existence.

Consequently Egyptian painting and sculpture provide us with a picture, severely stylized but essentially informative, of Egyptian life as it affected king and priest. And the hard rock out of which the sculptors carved their statues and the dry climate which was kind to the stone and pigment have preserved vast quantities of sculpture and painting. Our knowledge of Egyptian art is extraordinarily complete. Every brand of it from ladies' dressing-table equipment to colossal statues of Pharaohs can be studied in museums or in countless well-illustrated publications. There is no need, therefore, to attempt the thankless task of describing in detail a set of characteristics that must be well known to everyone who reads this book. Whatever its function—whether it is commemorating the majesty of Rameses II in a statue whose hand is bigger than a man, or describing the busy agricultural life of the Nile valley in a tomb painting, the art of Egypt is always dignified, almost always sensitive, technically superb, hardly ever vulgar, almost never playful or humorous. What it achieves (see Fig. 12) more than any other art is a serene, aloof, polished grandeur that survives even the mustiness of a museum setting. It is the perfect expression of a smoothly working, inexorable machine.

Only at one moment in its long service to state religion did it lose its character as the combination of robot and family butler. That was when, in the Eighteenth Dynasty, Akhenaton (the "heretic king") had the courage to revolutionize and humanize state religion. The result on the art of Egypt was rather as though the family retainer and his master had taken a week-end off in the country together, and the one had at last learned not to "keep his place" quite so correctly in the presence of the other. Sculpture took on, for a brief period, a new spirit. There is almost the equivalent of laughter in it, or if not of laughter, then of something deeper—enjoyment. But it was only a brief respite. Akhenaton's reign was a short and rather shocking experiment in freedom. Egyptian art soon hardened again into the overpowering highly stylized perfection that had characterized it for so many centuries.

Mesopotamian art is as old as that of Egypt. Its best-known form is that of Babylonia and Assyria. Here, as in Egypt, the artist was the official state propagandist, and had to work within a highly elaborated set of conventions. But the spirit of Babylon on the Euphrates and Nineveh on the Upper Tigris was very different from that of Egypt. All three were highly organized despotisms. In the case of all three one feels in the presence of a relentless organization, but whereas in Egypt it was productiveness and continuity that were organized, in Babylon and Nineveh it was power. It would not be difficult to find a modern counterpart to the creed of Mesopotamia. Lust for power and a merciless code in using and enforcing it give Mesopotamian sculpture an odd flavour. As in Egypt, it is entirely commemorative or descriptive, but its theme is conquest and the strength of the conqueror. The human body is lumpy and thick set, as though fitted only for the shooting of arrows and the hurling of javelins. It has none of the Egyptian leanness and litheness. The biceps and muscles of the calf are what attract one's attention. Women have hardly any place in it. Lions and bulls with human heads become symbols of this will-to-power.

It is a heavy, depressing art, technically skilful but completely earth-bound. To the archaeologist these records of military and kingly prowess must be fascinating. But if art is to be regarded either as a communication of the nobler aspects of the human spirit or as a means of creating formal harmony, then it must be admitted that if the later phases of Mesopotamian art had been destroyed the world would be little the poorer.

CHAPTER VII

THE ÆGEAN AND ATHENS

IT was in the Ægean Islands, with Crete as the centre of focus, that one can first see the beginnings of that restless visual curiosity that was to determine the course of European art. Doubtless the Cretans found their first inspiration in Egypt, but they did not feed it from Egypt. Behind almost all Egyptian art there is a sense of ceremonial; in Cretan art the men and women (especially the men) seem just to be having a good time; they are behaving like individuals. They are no longer performing parts allotted to them by the state machine. One can detect in their behaviour the beginnings of democracy. The frozen stylization and the refinement of Egyptian art have disappeared: so has the domination of king and religion. Cretan art radiates from neither the tomb nor the temple, but from the palace and the villa. The Cretan artist was more like the artist of to-day in that he seems to have chosen as his subject the things that pleased and attracted him, or caught his roving eye.

The civilization that centred in Crete spread itself widely along the Ægean coast. The most lively of the paintings are Cretan, but the man whose name is most closely linked with the age was not an artist, but a poet. Homer had no connection with Crete nor had Crete any part in Homeric legend, though the Cretan Minotaur and the Labyrinth were incorporated into Greek mythology. It is possible that while the Homeric sagas were crystallizing, the Cretan empire and the great palace of Cnossus had already succumbed to some nameless raider who had no Homer to celebrate his victory. The *Iliad* happens to deal with the Sack of Troy on the coast of Asia Minor by raiders from the Greek mainland. But Homer's picture of the Ægean way of life in the early part of the first millennium before Christ (his detailed descriptions of armour, for example) apply almost as closely to Crete as they do to Tiryns and Mycenæ, the home of Agamemnon on the Greek mainland, or to Ithaca, the home of Odysseus, or to Troy.

Compared with the enormous mass of painting and sculpture that survives from Egypt and Mesopotamia, what is left to us from the Cretan and Homeric age is fragmentary. Intrinsically it would hardly be worth more than a paragraph in so short an account of

European art. But its importance is not only intrinsic. It was the first beginning of an art-cycle that was to culminate in the age of Pericles and was to be killed in the end by Christianity, the cycle of which, as I have already suggested, the keyword was "physique." There are no important statues left from the Minoan age, but the little faience statuettes of priestesses found at Cnossus and the frescoes at Tiryns and Cnossus showing figures engaged on some kind of ritual are Egyptian only in their proud bearing. The women are tight-laced and they flaunt their bare breasts as though conscious for the first time of being individuals. The men, too, are not merely males. They carry their broad-shouldered, small-waisted bodies exultingly, like Russian ballet dancers. A famous gold cup from Vaphio shows these men hunting bulls as though they were engaged in sport rather than business. Any Egyptian artist would have given the impression that hunting bulls was part of the endless round of human duty. The Vaphio cup suggests that bull-hunting was rather a lark. A steatite vase from Crete shows a crowd of peasants singing as they return from harvesting. Here again the effect is of country bumpkins having a good time, and not of workmen doing what they had to do.

The most remarkable stylistic change in this breakaway from the Egyptian art machine is the attempt at foreshortening and perspective. The bulls on the Vaphio cup swing their heads toward the spectator, the harvesters are no longer severely pro-cessional. They are grouped casually, one behind the other, more like picnickers than an army on the march.

What remains of the palaces of Mycenæ and Tiryns suggests that they were destroyed by fire and siege. Little is known about the Greek invaders who destroyed them and ousted their occupants, but their art for all its inevit-able derivation from Homeric art was a cruder and more primitive affair. It was not spirited and gay, but intensely serious —the early Greek statues of athletes give an impression that the men who carved them had bitten off more than they could chew. They were trying to solve no less a problem than the complete and free representation of the naked human body for its own sake and not as hitherto for the sake of illustration or symbolism. The Cretans had solved their problem of depicting life and movement brilliantly and, as it were, instinctively, like born linguists who plunge courageously into speech before they have studied grammar. The early Hellenic sculptors make dogged and by no means brilliant attempts to learn the grammar of the human body before they try to make it speak. Their earliest statues of naked boys and girls dressed in a single simple garment, stand strictly to attention, staring into space with a meaningless smile that confines itself to their lips. These two types of adolescent are the only ones that interest the early Greek sculptor. It was a restricted field within which to work. The Greek artist never attempted to step outside it, but he was determined to exploit it to the full. Art to the Greek was a more specialized and restricted thing than it ever had been before, and for precisely the reason that to him life was a very full thing. Consumed with curiosity about his surroundings, not content merely to get on with the work like the Egyptians, or with the battle like the Assyrians, the Greek began to split his life into watertight compartments, and for each compartment he had a carefully elaborated mode of expression. For pure thought philosophy, for telling stories epic poetry, for emotional expression lyric poetry, and so on; he even imagined a sort of ministry of fine arts with its headquarters on Mount Parnassus and the nine Muses as heads of departments, though significantly enough painting and sculpture had no Muses.

The Greek theory that each art should be confined to its own department of experience, and that the province of painting and sculpture was to express the Greek admiration for physical perfection in the human adolescent and (later) in the human adult, was a specialist's theory, and with characteristic thoroughness the Greek began to work it out in practice.

Slowly these archaic Greek statues, looking at first as if they had been confined within coffins or the hollow trunks of trees, so cramped are their postures, and so rectangular or circular their cross-sections, begin to come to life. Very tentatively they advance the left foot, and in doing so they take on the exact position adopted by one type of Egyptian statue (see Figs. 12 and 13). But the effect is different. The Egyptian statue looks as if its maker knew all about the human figure and had deliberately stylized it. The Greek sculptor seems to be in perpetual difficulties. Pygmalion-like he does his best to bring his statue to life, to make it look natural. His eye searches out the beginning and end of each muscle, the boundaries of each plane, the formation of each lock of hair, and in his struggle to come to terms with each separate limb stylization creeps in against his will. The Egyptian statue stands easily and commandingly, like a man engaged in ceremonial who chooses to be motionless in order to add to his own dignity: the Greek is taut and holds its breath like a man sitting to an unkind photographer who insists on a half-minute exposure. One feels this desperate struggle and somehow one's heart is melted by it. There is a queer pathos about these early stone youths and maidens. They are not just nameless embodiments of dignity, like their Egyptian counterparts. They are real boys and girls—or they would have been had their makers only had the power to free them from their stone prisons. The Pygmalion myth takes on a new meaning in their presence. One is reminded of the pain caused by warm blood trying to circulate in a frostbitten finger.

Soon the girls manage to sit down, still rigidly staring into space, and those that remain standing take hold of a fold of the dress with the fingers and thumb of the left hand and twitch it delicately upwards. Over a period of two centuries the Greek sculptor plodded on like a slow-witted but conscientious school-boy determined to master his task however long it took him. And gradually he did master it. Gradually his figure began to thrust out an arm, turn its head, lean forward to make a spear-thrust or kneel on one knee to shoot an arrow. Not that the Greek sculptor was particularly interested in the shooting of arrows—that belonged to a different department: that was archery, not art—but that he wanted an excuse to show off his physically perfect adolescent. Moreover the low triangular pediment of the Greek temple provided a space which had to be filled with statues of different heights so that a mixture of standing, sitting, kneeling or recumbent poses was obligatory. Doubtless the Egyptian or Mesopotamian would have solved the pediment problem in another way, by varying the actual scale of the figures according to their social or religious importance. But such a procedure was contrary to the democratic spirit of Greece.

There is plenty of first-hand evidence about archaic Greek art. Statues of the Seventh and Sixth Centuries B.C. exist in large enough numbers to provide a firm basis of knowledge. But of the later stages in the development of Greek sculpture our knowledge is more fragmentary. Roman taste in sculpture was very like mid-Victorian taste. Rich Romans liked the mature, the rounded, the graceful, and after the downfall of Greece they carried the bulk of later Greek statuary (the collective noun somehow conveys their attitude) across to Italy as villa furniture, not scrupling to order copies of their favourite pieces and to re-emphasize their roundness and gracefulness in the copying. The later downfall of Rome completed the destruction and dispersal of Periclean and post-Periclean Greek carving, and to-day our available data are limited to fragments. What we know about Golden-age Greek sculpture is comparable to what we should know about Florentine painting if we possessed no original work by any artist from (and including) Botticelli to (and including) Michelangelo, with the exception of a fragment of a Raphael Madonna, a set of seventeenth-century engravings after Leonardo's pictures, a couple of bronze medals translating portions of the Sistine chapel ceiling into low relief and the upper half of Piero della Francesca's "Nativity." Doubtless this fragmentary evidence together with Vasari's Lives of the Painters and a host of documents about their dealings with their patrons would provide our art historians with an inexhaustible mine of speculation. The speculation would harden into legend, the legend into fact, until in the end we should feel that, though it was a pity to have lost so much, we had a pretty good idea of what the fine flower of late fifteenth and early sixteenth-century Florentine painting was like.

Moreover the taste of to-day, whetted by our later knowledge of negro sculpture, our sophisticated love of naïveté and our own experiments in a more angular set of rhythms, has swung away from maturity. That moment in the development of art when the initial set of problems has been solved, when the sense of struggle has given place to a sense of achievement, and the upward climb has been rewarded by a brief spell of basking on the summit is no longer the moment that interests us. It is a good moment to live in, but to those who, like ourselves, look back on it, it suggests a slackening of the tension, and a hint of smugness behind the achievement. Particularly does this apply to such of the Golden-age Greek art as has come down to us after passing through the sieve of Roman taste. The nature of the summit towards which the Greeks were toiling upwards is so familiar to us that it is no longer a matter of wonderment that they got there. We have seen the same kind of ascent to a higher summit achieved by the Italian painters. We know how they too made it their business to give their work "naturalness." We know the stages through which art has to pass on this journey. But the Italians had a much bigger task to accomplish. They were not only concerned with physique, as we shall see, but with a set of spiritual values which lay outside the Greek view of life.

What the Greek had to do in his progress from the naked seventh-century boys of the Acropolis to the technical perfection of the Elgin marbles is, to us, a foregone conclusion. Given the seedling and the flower in full bloom it would be perfectly easy for us to deduce the intermediate stages even if we had no evidence at all. The Greek artist had three things to learn. He had to learn to see his statue in the round instead of from the front only: he had to study movement as well as anatomy; he had to see his figure as a whole instead of a sum of parts. Those three problems are the problems common to all art-development. In addition there were the self-imposed problems that were peculiarly Greek, of making the type as beautiful as possible and of avoiding the suggestion of individuality. For individuality implies a departure from the norm, the one thing to be avoided if your aim is physical perfection.

All that art historians can tell us is the names of the sculptors who contributed most to this development. There was Myron who specialised in movement and made a bronze statue of the discus-thrower well known through Roman marble copies. Myron was evidently far in advance of his time. The "Discobolus" still clings to the "frontality" conception (i.e. one feels that there is one "best" point of view from which to view it) but the twist of the torso is done with complete assurance. There was Polycleitus who specialized in physical beauty and grace of posture and is said to have produced a statue called the Canon or Standard in which the proportions were so "correct" that no sculptor who copied them could go wrong. There was Pheidias to whom tradition assigns the supervision (though not the execution) of the Parthenon carvings and who is supposed to have been a master of restrained nobility of gesture. There was Praxiteles (his "Hermes" is the only surviving Greek statue assignable to a known Greek sculptor) who gave his statues more charm, and a little more individuality than his predecessors. There was Lysippus (court sculptor to Alexander the Great) who gave the human figure a new suppleness. At this point (say 350 B.C.) it can be said that all technical difficulties have been solved and that a Greek sculptor is now capable of doing with bronze or marble exactly what he likes. What he *did* like varied with the sculptor. Some of it, like the famous Laocoön group or the frieze from the altar of Zeus at Pergamon, strikes the Twentieth Century as a wild and rather vulgar display of virtuosity which could have been outdone by many a baroque sculptor of the Seventeenth Century. Some of it, like the Victory of Samothrace, or the lovely relief of Victory bending to tie her sandal is felicitous in design: some of it, like the statues of Niobe and her children, is just boring.

I am conscious that this chapter on Greek art is written with a lack of enthusiasm that makes it dull reading. The fact is that the flavour of mature Greek sculpture, in the form it has come down to us, does seem to me an uninspiring thing, though isolated examples of it are undeniably noble and others are undeniably

tender. Nevertheless these isolated examples seem to me to have
nothing to do with the Greek sculptor's main objective. They are
brilliant exceptions—almost lapses. The weakness, to me, of the
whole of the Greek theory of sculpture is that it was pursuing an
aim that was attainable. Beyond a certain point nothing more
could be done. It was heading, along a difficult and fascinating
road, straight for a *cul-de-sac*. It took three and a half centuries
to reach the end and, having reached it, it was bound to perish,
not as other schools of painting and sculpture have perished, from
a slackening of tension in the artist's own vision, but because it
had literally accomplished all it set out to do. It had attained
perfection, the most dangerous thing that a human being can
attain, for perfection brings immobility and immobility implies
death. Greek sculpture is linked up with nothing in human
experience beyond the physical. When we see a headless Greek
statue we do not wonder what the head was like: we know that
the head would tell us nothing. It would not alter the statue's
mood, for the statue has hardly any mood. An armless Greek
Venus is not incomplete; it arouses no curiosity as to what she
was doing with her arms. We know perfectly well she was doing
nothing. She was just being Venus—and even that in the mildest
way. Physical love is an intense thing; it provided Greek tragedy
with one of its bloodiest themes, and yet the statue of the Cnidian
Aphrodite can boast no more than physical perfection. She has
no intensity. She is in essence no more than the perfect chorus
girl. If we knew the Greek way of life only through their sculpture
we should judge them an unemotional race whose interests were
largely centred in the gymnasium. Knowing them as we do, from
their literature, I cannot help regretting that more of the intense
intellectual activity it reflects was not carried over into their art.

The Greek sculptors did one thing only and did it so superbly
that it has left its mark on the whole history of European art.
They established a canon of human beauty and human nobility
from which, until Gauguin went to Tahiti to search for a new
norm, no European artist ever thought of departing. In Greek
art Man and God are indistinguishable, for they depend not on
their function but on their appearance.

I have no wish to debunk Greek sculpture. An art that could
produce carvings as charming as the flute players on the Ludovisi
throne, as noble as the three Fates on the Parthenon Pediment,
as rhythmical as the Niké tying her sandal or one or two of the
Athenian funeral Stelæ cannot be debunked. It makes too deep
an impression on our visual experience for that. My contention

is merely that Greek art, by excluding from its province what is known as the human soul, set itself a task that could be, and was, completely and perfectly accomplished. It headed all the time for a point well within human reach, and the journey to that point was more interesting than the arrival. Was Pygmalion, once he had brought his Galatea to life, crushed to death in her arms?

If there is little enough of mature Greek sculpture left to us there is nothing at all of Greek painting, but it is not difficult to imagine its characteristics and limitations. From contemporary writers one gathers that it aimed at realism of light and shade as well as of detail: that "finish" and precision were admired qualities. From the comparative inability of even the best Greek sculptors to group their statues in satisfactory relation to each other one could guess at an elementary type of composition, a guess that is borne out by the few frescoes that remain from Roman villas painted under Greek influence. Except in the realm of portraiture Rome had nothing to add to what Greece had already said. She copied Greek forms, but without their restraint, and imitated Greek grace but with an added dose of sweetness.

CHAPTER VIII

BYZANTINE, ROMANESQUE AND GOTHIC

No period in the history of European civilization is more obscure than that which saw the slow break up of the Roman Empire. Men must have worked, eaten, built houses, written books, sung songs, carved statues and painted images during those few centuries we call the Dark Ages, but it is difficult to picture them at it. There seems to be no centre of focus, no peg on which to hang our thoughts about those queer, flavourless centuries. Rome was dead as a cultural centre of gravity, the pagan gods were moribund. Christianity was a growing power but an underground power; it had not yet become, as it was to become later, a magnet round which every form of human activity, good and bad, could revolve. What was life like in the Fourth Century A.D. in St. Albans, Aix-en-Provence or Athens? What clothes did the men wear, how did the women dress their hair? It is no use asking the antiquarian such questions. He will answer them, but our mental picture will be no clearer for his answers. An artistic vacuum had occurred, and one realizes for the first time how dependent on the art of a period is one's mental picture of the period.

A vacuum can be filled only if material for filling it is ready to hand, and at this blank moment between the shrivelling of paganism and the budding of Christianity such material did not exist. Art needs a harness, and during this dead interval of time there was nothing for the artist to harness himself to. Even in places where Christianity had already taken root he could do nothing, for the language he had been accustomed to use, the language of physique, could not be made to apply to the new creed. If art was to serve Christianity it must evolve a new language—a symbolic language to replace the old descriptive one.

As long as Christianity had no official status it could produce no art. In the Roman catacombs a few tentative experiments in evolving the new symbolism were made, but they are of little æsthetic interest. There was, however, one exception to the confusion that reigned over most of Europe. There was a patch that was comparatively peaceful and comparatively civilized round the eastern end of the Mediterranean. Syria, Asia Minor and Egypt formed an area within which, given favourable circumstances, the new art could develop. It needed the stimulus of a state-protected religion, and the consequent appearance of a set of state-approved churches to give such art a dwelling-place.

It was at this moment that the pendulum that had swung steadily from Egypt to Crete, from Crete to Greece, and from Greece to Rome, stopped swinging and hung in the balance, waiting for the advent of a fresh impulse to send it back. If the impulse can be attributed to a single man, that man is the Emperor Constantine who had the good sense to choose this moment (A.D. 330) to move eastwards into the area that still showed signs of civilization, and to transfer the seat of the Empire to Constantinople, and at the same time to adopt a protective and tolerant attitude towards Christianity. At last it was possible for Christian art to attach itself to something permanent—to the church wall. There it could find a home for itself more fitting than the art of Egypt had ever found in the tomb, or the art of Greece in the temple. The art of Egypt belonged to the tomb only in the sense that a bundle of share certificates belong to a fireproof safe; and Greek statues had only belonged to the temple in the sense that framed pictures belong to a room. But early Christian art belongs to the church as the text of a book belongs to the paper on which it is printed. The Christian artist had an opportunity given to no other artist before him—the opportunity of *creating* a complete iconography of the visual side of religion, and not merely of *illustrating* it. It was an opportunity almost too big for any man to grasp, and at first it was done fumblingly. If it had been left to Rome to do it, it would have been badly done. All Rome could do was to apply worn-out pagan symbols to the new religion, to depict an Apollo or an Orpheus and label him Jesus, or to make Christ and His disciples look (as they do in the early mosaic of S. Pudenziana in Rome) rather like an informal meeting of the Senate. Fortunately the Oriental section of the Empire was much better fitted for the task. Even before Christianity had been recognized, a mysticized version of paganism (known as Mithraism) had been developing in Egypt, Syria and Asia Minor, and it was easy enough to adapt this mystical frame of mind to Christianity. It is difficult to fix a precise date at which the pendulum can be said to have turned back. One of the earliest major works of Christian art is the mausoleum of Galla Placidia at Ravenna of the fourth century. Here, in a tiny brick building no bigger than a country cottage, the Roman idioms are used with a purely Oriental effect. The Saints look like Roman philosophers, the beardless Christ is nothing but a rustic shepherd sitting in rather vapid bucolic contentment among his sheep, and yet to enter the brick shell and to find oneself in an unearthly gloom encrusted with blue and silver and gold mosaics is to be taken at a leap right across the Greek peninsula into an atmosphere that only a semi-oriental vision could have conceived. This is the earliest successful attempt to serve up the old pagan wine in the new Christian bottle. The pendulum has begun to swing, but only just. A more spectacular impulse was given to it by the building of the great church of Santa Sophia in Constantinople by the Emperor Justinian and his pious ex-actress wife Theodora. I am not here concerned with the church as a landmark in architectural construction, and the mosaics which cover its interior are only now being freed from the coat of whitewash with which Islam insisted on covering them after the Turkish occupation of Constantinople, so that it is too early to point to them as prototype of Eastern Byzantine art. But Justinian erected an equally significant though smaller example of sixth-century Byzantine art in the church of San Vitale in Ravenna. Here the new symbolism is beginning to gain the upper hand. The Roman idioms are still there but they have ceased to count for much. They are supplanted by a new orchestral use of colour. Colour, treated by the Egyptians and Greeks merely as a useful descriptive or decorative addition, is here used for full-blooded emotional ends. What is significant about this building and its host of successors is that it was regarded, architecturally, as a set of interior wall-spaces. It was built from the inside outwards. It had no significance whatever until you entered it. The Greek temple was a thing of deliberate self-contained beauty, to be looked at from the outside, a thing which a little added sculpture would certainly improve, but which could easily survive the absence of it. The church of San Vitale is a blank brick book whose pages are meaningless until they have been lined with mosaic. The Christian artist was being given his opportunity with a vengeance.

The new attitude to mosaic is of the utmost significance. Mosaic was not an unknown medium before the Byzantine era, but it had been thought of by the Greeks and Romans as a means of decorating a surface unsuitable for paint—a floor where paint would have been worn away, or the inside of a fountain, where paint would have been washed off. But now it became not only a structural part of the wall, but the *raison d'être* for the wall. The wall was built for the sole purpose of holding it up, and windows were pierced in the wall for the sole purpose of illuminating it.

Mosaic, unlike paint, is a rigid, inflexible medium; it imposes a fierce discipline on the artist who uses it. The Romans, who used it in places where paint was unsuitable, tried to make it express painterly ideas, and the early Christian artists of the West (see the upper panels of Sant' Apollinare Nuovo in Ravenna) continued so to use it. Even in San Vitale, where the general effect is remote and unearthly, the two famous groups of Justinian and his ecclesiastical attendants and soldiers on one side and of Theodora with her handmaidens on the other are relics of a Roman view of life in which the Emperor was more important than the church, and the earth was as worthy of the artist's attention as the heavens. But as the Byzantine pendulum continued to swing, and as the influence of the Eastern group of artists spread, mosaic began to be used as it should be used, as the perfect vehicle for visual symbolism on a large scale. William Morris once said it was like beer in that it was no good unless you had a lot of it. In the churches of Parenzo on the Adriatic opposite to Ravenna (sixth century), of Sant' Agnese in Rome (seventh century), Santa Prassede in Rome (ninth century), at Daphne, near Athens (eleventh century), at Cefalú, in the Capella Palatina and in the Cathedral of Monreale in Sicily (twelfth century), in St. Mark's, Venice (mainly thirteenth and fourteenth centuries), to pick out a handful of typical examples from a host of others, what counts for as much as the quality of the design and the richness of the colour is the sheer profusion of the mosaic. It is overpowering, as a big Bach fugue is overpowering, through its cumulative effect. Some of it is not particularly interesting in detail, but almost always it is impressive in its general planning, in the placing of its climaxes and in its genius for being glowing and remote at the same time.

From the dates of the churches in the list given above, it will be seen that as the chief vehicle for Christian propaganda it lasted for about eight centuries. Throughout that period the Byzantine pendulum continued to swing in a fashion that belies all the accepted theories of art development. The idea that an art cycle progresses from primitive to mature, and from mature to decadent: that the primitive period is one in which the expression of emotional sincerity interferes with the discovery of visual truth, that the decadent period is one in which visual truth has killed emotional sincerity and that the mature period is one in which sincerity and truth are happily married—this delightfully simple theory is not borne out by the history of Byzantine art. It is only on the forward swing of the pendulum, the Discobolus-Laocoön swing, or the Giotto-Cézanne swing, that this happens. The backward swing is governed by a different set of laws. It is not that the process is reversed. It is a different process. It begins, as we have seen, by a deliberate breakaway from the realism that had come before it, necessitated by the fact that realism will no longer serve the purpose of the new art cycle. It works its way gradually to a set of forms so remote from visual experience, so engendered by a state of mind, that it becomes almost purely abstract. And finally these abstract forms gradually harden into a set of artistic clichés and become incapable of further development. They are valid only as long as the ideas they express are valid. In the Byzantine case this schematization was imposed on the artist from above, so that from being the creator of a mystical mood he became the illustrator of a series of incidents for the benefit of an illiterate people. Types of these three periods of development in the Byzantine cycle are (1) the upper portions of the sides of the apse of San Vitale (sixth century), where a beardless Moses standing on an impossibly symbolic mountain watches the hand of God emerge from impossibly romantic clouds; (2) the wall above the apse of Santa Prassede, Rome (ninth century), where the twenty-four elders stand in a pattern more formal, more violently distorted, from the point of view of visual truth, than anything Picasso has ever dared to attempt with the human

1. Giotto. *Arena Chapel, Padua.* Detail

2. Grünewald.
The Crucifixion, Colmar.
Detail

VARIATIONS

ON A THEME

3. Russian. (School of Rublev)

4. Sienese. (Simone Martini)

5. Florentine. (Raphael)

6. Late Venetian. (Tiepolo)

7. Sung Dynasty. *Ladies preparing silk.* Detail

EASTERN CONTEMPLATION &

丹槲青松蓋
草扉浮光不
動鏡光滿凄
稜稜家相摸
遠等度秋風
一到談
花溪已己秋
佈題

9. Chinese Landscape

8. Courbet. *La Toilette de la Mariée*. Detail

WESTERN VISUAL CURIOSITY

10. Constable.
The Lock Gates

11. Byzantine. (Salonika)

14. Romanesque. (Chartres)

12. Egyptian   13. Archaic Greek

15. Italian Renaissance (Pollaiuolo: detail from *The Martyrdom of St. Sebastian*)

16. Flemish (Pieter Brueghel: *The Village Wedding*)

17. Andrea del Castagno.   Detail

18.
Leonardo da Vinci.
Detail from cartoon by
d'Oggione

9. Venetian. (Titian)

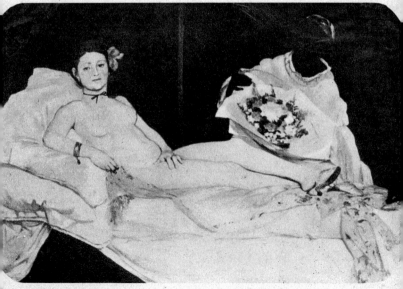

20. Parisian. (Manet)

21. El Greco. *The Burial of Count Orgaz*

22. Rubens. *The Assumption*

23. Velasquez

24. Rembrandt

25. Terborch. *The Guitar Lesson*

6. Madox Brown.
The Last of England
y Permission of the
Museum and Art Gallery
Committee of the Cor-
oration of Birmingham

27. Monet. *Rouen Cathedral*

28. Renoir. *Baigneuse*

29. Cézanne. *Gardanne*

30. Picasso. *Still Life*

31. Michelangelo

32. Henry Moore

figure; (3) the mosaics in the domes of the Narthex of St. Mark's, Venice (thirteenth century), in which the story of Genesis is told in concentric circles, each divided into square compartments like a modern comic strip. The first is a half-hearted attempt to depict an actual scene by a man who is not interested in actuality, but cannot think how to dispense with it; the second is pure symbolism without a thought for actuality; the third is an attempt to use symbolism for the purposes of narrative by a man who has been out of touch with actuality for seven centuries, but whose employers are beginning to demand it once more.

During the whole of this period no name emerges, no mosaicist of genius whom one can point to as having produced the perfect flower of Byzantine art. It is an anonymous art. Even more than in Egypt is the artist submerged in his task and even more than in Egypt is he compelled to work within a set of established formulæ. He is serving a cause, not exploiting his personality. For this very reason it is not easy to write the history of Byzantine art. To do so is like trying to make a map of a wide landscape with a distinctive flavour of its own but without milestones or landmarks. Its course is marked by none of those discoveries that the typical European artist always tries to make and which the art historian delights to record. It is as little capable of being translated into words as a melody; and, worse still, it almost refuses to be translated into reproduction. A photograph of an Egyptian statue gives one a fairly accurate sense of the original, a photograph of a fresco by Giotto or a painting by Velasquez supply more information about the originals than pages of laboured description. But a photograph of the interior of the church at Cefalú bears as little relation to the church itself as a Walt Disney drawing of Donald Duck does to a Donald Duck cartoon. Figure 11 shows a portion of a dome in Salonika. It illustrates perhaps the boldness of Byzantine formalism, but it fails to convey Byzantine impressiveness. Add to this the unfortunate fact that Byzantine mosaics are not portable and that no important examples exist within several hundreds of miles of this country and it becomes plain that to write an adequate account of this—by far the most important—aspect of Byzantine art is almost impossible. And yet, to me, the whole corpus of Byzantine mosaic from the Sixth to the Twelfth Century is one of the most deeply moving of all manifestations of the human spirit. I regret my powerlessness as a writer to communicate its flavour. My only alternative would be to describe in detail the iconographical laws that governed it and the technical problems involved in mosaic making. And that, I feel, is not worth doing in so short a book. Students can find out elsewhere how the "Last Judgment" had to be represented in five superimposed layers, how Denys of Fourna prescribes who are the proper persons to be included in representations of the "Dormition of the Virgin," and what positions they may occupy; how tesseræ of glass and marble were fixed into their bed of mastic, and how gold-leaf was fused between an upper and a lower layer of transparent glass. The whole of the later Byzantine era was characterized by a respect for tradition in both iconography and craftsmanship. The level of craftsmanship in ivory carving, low relief sculpture (the Byzantine decorative genius was essentially two-dimensional: sculpture in the round was outside its scope), metal-work and jewellery and the painting of miniatures, frescoes and ikons was remarkably high.

The influence of Byzantine mannerisms was widespread in the East. All over the Balkans, especially in the area that was once Serbia, provincial schools of fresco painting took root, but the only form of Byzantine painting that need concern us here is the painting of ikons which developed so surprisingly late and continued for so long in Russia.

When Constantinople passed into Mohammedan keeping it was Russia who became heir, as it were, to the Byzantine view of life, and the forms which for centuries had ceased to mean anything in Europe became the central Russian tradition and took on a new life. Again, it is an anonymous art, and though provincial schools of ikon painters developed slightly different ways of treating the given themes, the only famous name among the painters of ikons is that of Rublev, a monk of the Spaco-Andrankov Monastery in Moscow. The Madonna and Child shown in Figure 3 shows how simple and intense in feeling the ikon could be at its best, and though as far as design is concerned the whole school seems to have developed out of itself (it is the only example I know of art based on art that did not immediately perish for lack of outside stimulus), the harmonization and distribution of colour in the average ikon are among the most adventurous and subtle experiments in the history of painting.

So much for the eastern half of Europe. Meanwhile the continued social and political chaos in the western half made it impossible for a parallel set of traditions to evolve until much later. Again, the development of a western European art was dependent on the building of churches. In the East there was no break in output between the final collapse of Rome and the rise of Constantinople, but in the West there occurred a real hiatus filled only by the carving of a few stone crosses in Northumberland and on the Scottish border, or by a few illuminated manuscripts from Ireland or from Central Europe. One has to wait for what we have agreed to call rather meaninglessly the Romanesque type of architecture in order to give the representational arts a new *point d'appui*.

Christmas Day, A.D. 800, when Charlemagne attended Mass in St. Peter's at Rome and was crowned by the Pope as head of the Holy Roman Empire, was a significant day. Not that anything resembling unity in Western Europe was accomplished by the symbolic event, but after the year A.D. 800 there was at least a potential rallying force for Western European culture as soon as it was ready to emerge. Charlemagne himself was an unashamed eclectic who could think of nothing better to do for art than to produce a stone church in Aix la Chapelle based on San Vitale in Ravenna, to hire Byzantine mosaicists to fill it with decorations which have long since disappeared, and to base his ornamental motives on Irish illuminated manuscripts. It was not till the beginning of the Eleventh Century, 200 years after the establishment of the Holy Roman Empire, that Romanesque architecture had evolved its own language.

It was a language of stone—a three-dimensional language, whereas Byzantine was a language of brick, coated with two-dimensional decorations. Like Byzantine art, the main body of it is " applied " art. It belongs to the building and cannot be divorced from it. But being conceived in stone it consists largely of sculpture. Generally speaking, the nearer it approaches to the East the more apt it is to emphasize surface and take the form of low relief; the further West it penetrates, the solider and more fully rounded it becomes. But whether it is in low relief and consequently conceived as line, or sculpture in the round and therefore conceived as mass, it is essentially an art in which form counts rather than colour. This, of course, is roughly true of all European as opposed to Oriental art, but the history of Romanesque art and its development into Gothic art (there seems no adequate reason to separate the two: they are phases of the same movement) is essentially the history of an art whose main concern was with *shape*.

What is more noteworthy still is that it is an art with no centre of radiation, no main stream traceable to a definite source such as Nineveh or Cnossus or Athens had been. If ever there was a period when one could speak of a United States of Europe it was this period between the fall of Rome and the re-centring of European culture in Italy. In Mediæval Europe national boundaries were so fluid and national consciousness so weak that cultural movements found no difficulty in flowing freely across them. Consequently one can find fully developed expressions of the Romanesque and Gothic spirit in almost any corner of Europe at any moment. The façade of the Church of St. Trophime at Arles in Provence, of the Cathedral of Chartres in North-Western France (see Fig. 14), of the Cathedral of Santiago in Spain, of the Church of San Zeno in Verona are all variations on the same theme. Romanesque and Gothic art are dependent on the vast organization of the Catholic Church and not on the inspiration of a geographical centre as Florence was to be later and as Paris was until the spring of 1940.

As in Byzantine art, the output is enormous but anonymous. And, as in Byzantine art, what we have to examine is a slowly changing mood rather than a succession of independent masterpieces. What characterizes the whole Romanesque movement is a perfect co-ordination between the carving and its architectural setting. The spacing of the statues on the façade of Saint Trophime, the richness of their surface contrasted with the smooth stone wall above them, the manner in which they alternate rhythmically with the supporting columns of the overhanging porch, the distribution of the shadows, the controlled freedom of line give the eye a thrill of satisfaction. There is nothing profound in Romanesque carving, but it invented a set of rhythms and textures which make archaic Greek sculpture look pedestrian by comparison. In no other period can one find such masses of carving, affectionate and meticulous in detail, yet held together by a breadth of design that includes the whole carved area and enables the eye to take it in at a single glance.

"Gothic" is a word with a queer history and even queerer connotations. Naturally the builders of Chartres or Canterbury had never heard the word. They may have thought of themselves as moderns (as compared with the builders of St. Trophime or Durham), but they would have been surprised to know that four centuries later men of culture looking for a word to describe their style would choose one that was synonymous with barbarous—as we to-day use the word Vandal. It is equally odd that Sir Henry Wotton could use the adjective in this derogatory way and that two and a half centuries later Ruskin could use it to imply the highest praise.

To the average man it implies neither scorn nor praise: it is just a technical term for the kind of building in which the arches are pointed. Or ask the average man to go a little deeper and ignore pedantic tests of this kind and he will tell you rather hesitatingly that he supposes the Gothic style is on the whole a vertical style whereas the Romanesque style is a horizontal style. And he will be correct as far as he goes. But if he suggests that vertical and horizontal are two irreconcilable systems of thought and that the first was the result of a sudden act of rebellion against the second, he will be wrong. Architecturally the possible shades of transition from Romanesque to Gothic and even from Byzantine to Gothic are infinite. Venice is full of buildings that are Gothic by definition, but Byzantine in spirit. The pointed arches of Monreale are more closely related to Byzantium than the round arches of Durham.

This book, however, is not concerned with buildings or arches, but with representations in paint and stone. If the word Gothic has any permanent meaning it must be applicable not only to a cathedral, but to a statue or a painting. Isolate an angel from the cathedral of Rheims, remove the Chichester roundel from its architectural context and how is one to know whether they are Gothic or not ? There is no neat answer to such questions. Gothic is a relative, not an absolute term. It is a flavour that can be either hardly detectable or, in extreme cases, overwhelming. What began to produce the flavour was another outburst of that spirit of visual curiosity which I have more than once said is among the chief motive forces of European art. Curiosity about the human body had produced Greek art; another kind of curiosity was responsible for the Gothic spirit. Greek curiosity was that of a scientist : Gothic curiosity was that of a lover. It was an affectionate curiosity, full of little whimsies and extravagancies. Instead of limiting itself to humanity it could range playfully and capriciously across the whole of creation, picking out details, a monstrous form here, a charming turn of the wrist there. Greece had developed in the direction of greater breadth and simplicity: Gothic developed in the direction of complexity and preciousness, and gaily mingled the grotesque with the elegant. It is this mixture that gives it its true flavour, and for that reason it can be summed up in no single statue or painting. If Byzantine mosaic is like beer in that one needs a lot of it, Gothic art is like a cocktail in that its separate ingredients do not fairly represent its final flavour. It has all the complexity of life itself.

"Romantic" is the obvious word for it, but that hardly helps, for "romantic," like "beautiful," is a word that will not survive the process of definition. To see Gothic at its impressive best one goes, of course, to the great cathedrals, especially the cathedrals of Northern France. But to see it at its most typical and intimate (for intimacy is one of its most endearing characteristics) one must study the illuminated manuscripts that were poured out from the Scriptoria of the various monasteries from the beginning of the Thirteenth Century: Books of Hours, Missals, Apocalypses, Psalters and Bibles. In them the Gothic artist, no longer a mere contributor to the architectural ensemble, can unleash his fancy and indulge all his whims. The figures are sometimes elongated to the verge of caricature, like fashion drawings of to-day (see the second part of the Arundel Psalter in the British Museum): grotesque creatures, humorous or macabre touches abound. As the type develops it becomes more restless. The eye is not given a moment's peace. Diaper backgrounds, borders of ivy leaves made even more spiky than nature had designed them, later on landscape backgrounds (about the middle of the Fifteenth Century), with clumps of elaborate flowers in the foreground, scenes from contemporary life, sports and pastimes, feasting, travelling, cooking (the Luttrell Psalter of 1340 in the British Museum is crowded with such miniatures) can be found everywhere. One would think that in the Fourteenth Century life in North-West Europe was one vast confusion of gay delightful detail, a nursery packed with living toys.

Oddly enough the style in which these miniatures are executed remains formal and stylized up to the middle of the Fifteenth Century. The passionate Gothic curiosity about *things* left the artist no time or thought for a parallel curiosity about *appearances*. One would have expected that this questing Gothic spirit would have led to discoveries of perspective, of light and shade, and that Romanticism would have given way to realism long before it did. It is not till the second half of the Fifteenth Century that research into appearances ousts research into *things* and that the word Gothic finally loses its meaning in the Northern section of Europe. Giotto had been dead four years when the Luttrell Psalter was being decorated.

One other manifestation of the Gothic spirit was the development of the stained glass window, and this in its turn was the result of a discovery in engineering—the discovery of the vaulted roof supported not by walls but by pillars. Having learned how to build a roof without walls, the Gothic architect was free to do what he liked with the spaces between the pillars, the areas which hitherto had been filled by walls. The discovery could never have been made in Southern Europe. where one of the architect's duties was to keep the strong sunlight out. In the North he needed all the light he could get, and he welcomed the opportunity of turning his new dummy walls into window frames. What the wall was to the Byzantine the window became to the Northern Gothic builder—an excuse for introducing colour. Here the Gothic artist was faced with a problem similar to that of the Byzantine mosaicist. He had to work in a medium that imposed its own laws on him. Smallish pieces of coloured transparent glass held together by narrow bands of lead made an excellent basis for colour decoration but were incapable of producing realism. The problem was one of pattern and colour-organization with a minimum of representational accuracy or narrative interest. Naturally iconography could not be kept out, for the church demanded it, but one cannot feel that the stained-glass craftsmen of the Thirteenth Century took their icono-graphical duties very seriously. It is impossible to regard the windows of Chartres as an illustrated Bible, as one can easily do in the case of the contemporary mosaics in the Narthex of St. Mark's in Venice. In Chartres the colour is too intense, the patterning too insistent. One cannot comfortably "read" Gothic windows. One has to let them evoke a mood. They do so quite overpoweringly, but since the representational factor plays so small a part in their impact on the senses they can be justifiably ignored in this account of Gothic art. By the time artists had learned to treat the window as a surface to paint a picture on the Gothic spirit was dead.

CHAPTER IX

FLORENCE, SIENA AND VENICE

It is at this point that the art historian settles himself comfort-ably in his chair, projects his mind to Assisi somewhere about the year 1290 when Giotto, aged twenty-four, is busy on the frescoes in the Church of St. Francis, takes out his pen and addresses himself to his task with a sense of relief. Everything is now plain sailing. The Renaissance is within sight. From 1290 till the present day the course of European painting is clear. Hardly a decade will pass without some famous name to fill it, some masterpiece familiar to a million readers. In 1290 the foundations of modern art were being sketched out and the shape of the whole structure was becoming inevitable, and what is more to the point for the art-historian, describable. There is a full technical vocabulary ready to his hand. The story has been written a thousand times, and who am I that I should shrink from writing it again?

It starts, unlike the story of every other art-cycle, with a giant. Giotto did for Florentine painting what Myron did for Greek sculpture. But he did it at the very beginning instead of profiting by a century of experiment. He suddenly saw life in the round. Painting, after 1300, needed no longer be an exercise in two-dimensional design; it could be an adequate representation of objects in space, objects that possessed not only shape and colour but weight and volume.

Here it is worth while to digress for a moment in order to enquire into the mechanism of evolution in the arts. I have suggested that during what I have called the forward swings of the pendulum the artist is obsessed with a desire to come to grips with appearances, to concern himself with what he would call visual truth as opposed to symbolic truth on the one hand and to visual harmony on the other. In theory it ought to be one of the artist's easiest tasks: on the face of it there is nothing to prevent him "copying" nature with the utmost accuracy whenever he wishes to. The eyesight of the sculptor who carved the archaic boys and girls of the Acropolis was presumably remarkably similar to the eyesight of Praxiteles, and the eyesight of Giotto to that of Rembrandt. Looking at the same object, all four would presumably have much the same image on the retina. How comes it, then, that the first pair produce entirely different statues and the second pair entirely different pictures? How is the stylistic difference between Greek sculpture of the Seventh Century B.C. and of the Fourth Century B.C. to be explained? Presuming that your archaic Greek sculptor is doing his best to fashion a stone image of a naked man exactly as his eyes see him (and the supposition seems reasonable in view of the later developments of Greek art), how does one account for the fact that any given statue of the period bears a much closer resemblance to any other statue of the same period than either of them does to the object represented? Why cannot sculptor B, noting the stiffness and immobility of sculptor A's attempt to carve a male athlete, and the system of frontality from which A seems unable to escape, why cannot he immediately carve a statue that has none of these "defects," merely using his eyes and his chisel to carve exactly what he sees? The answer appears to be that the eye is, as it were, one end of a complicated passage, at the other end of which the brain stands on guard refusing to admit anything with which it is not already familiar. The eye admits the whole visible world in a chaotic torrent of undigested visual information. But before the artist can deal with the information so admitted it must be sorted out. Now at any given moment in the development of vision, only certain limited quantities or aspects of that information are acceptable. What *is* acceptable at once becomes the artist's visual raw material, what is *not* is unusable and is therefore automatically rejected. It is useless for the artist to intellectualize the problem and to tell himself that the whole visible world in all its aspects is at his disposal. The sentry in his brain stands on guard in spite of him. In Leonardo's notebooks are long analyses of the nature and colour of light which, if he could have acted upon them, would have led to his painting with the palette of the nineteenth-century Impressionists. But Leonardo, giant though he was, could not *visualize* the conclusions to which his intellect had led him. He could *see* exactly what Monet and Pissarro saw, and he could *think* clearly enough to anticipate the Nineteenth Century, but the invisible sentry in his brain would admit nothing into his visual experience that was not already part of the common visual experience of the late Fifteenth Century. His vision would not travel at the same speed as his thought.

Period-vision can only develop by gradually persuading the unseen sentry that such and such aspects of what the eye has let through are respectable and trustworthy. They must arrive with proper credentials, and the highest credential they can have is that they have been used already by other artists and have passed into the accredited currency of art. To admit anything that is not part of contemporary currency is to take grave risks, and it is the mark of the adventurous spirit in art to be prepared to take such risks. Most artists will take infinitesimally small risks of this kind, and then only under the influence of a strong æsthetic emotion that positively beats down the sentry's defences.

In the whole history of art I can think of no painter who has taken more of these risks than Giotto, none who was less dependent on the artistic formulas of his time, none who made possible so long a stride forward in period-vision. For that reason he is the art-historian's most cherished figure, for he makes an unmistakable starting point for a new epoch in art-history. Florentine painting starts, like a sprint, with a pistol shot. In 1280 it hardly exists. By 1300 it is racing ahead. In fact it is racing ahead altogether too fast. Usually when a great artist has the audacity to admit a new set of visual experiences and embody them in his art, his followers are only too ready to profit by his daring. Within a few years his discoveries are already part of the tradition of his time. But here was a man who had gone ahead too far for his followers to catch him up. Or perhaps he came too early in the scene. The pistol shot went off, as it were, before the other runners knew that a race was in progress.

I have tried in the preceding chapter to describe the rigid Byzantine formula current at the end of the Thirteenth Century in Italy. It was as complete as the church could make it. Not only were the permissible subjects for Christian iconography carefully tabulated, but their order of precedence, the manner of their presentation, and even the colours to be used. Giotto, in breaking all these rules, was not quite alone, though he was alone in the world of painting. It was St. Francis who made the first attempt to break the iron chains in which Christian dogma had deliberately fettered itself. St. Francis in humanizing religion doubtless gave Giotto the courage to humanize art. These two innovations, the new capacity to see life in the round, and the new desire to infuse warmth into the chilly Byzantine conception of religion were opposite sides of the same medal. Giotto could conceivably have introduced either into his painting without the other, and either taken by itself would have made him an important figure. But his power to combine the two made him gigantic. His command of the three-dimensional world was a by-product of his humanity and, in particular, of his sense of human drama.

He regarded himself as a narrative painter. His concern was to tell his story by establishing the emotional relationship between the persons depicted in his frescoes. Now it may be said that this is already fully accomplished in the Russian Madonna and Child (Fig. 3). But it is done in a different spirit. If I simplify the ikon painter's problem by saying that his task is to find a set of visual symbols for the idea contained in the word

"tenderness," it must be admitted that he has solved the problem
and penetrated to the very core of the idea. Giotto could do that
too, but it was not enough. He then proceeded to project *himself*
in the orbit of the idea. Without losing any of the intensity of
the symbol he translated it into terms of life. What had been
disembodied became embodied. The spirit of tenderness began
to inhabit the tangible Madonna and Child of his own imagination. Every figure in Giotto's œuvre is, so to speak, an agent of
the emotion, a vessel specially created to contain it, so that
however "badly drawn" (according to academic standards) it
may be it is still performing its complete function. One has the
same feeling in reading Shakespeare. Psychologically his characters are so intensely and completely realized that the arbitrary
and often absurd behaviour they indulge in passes unnoticed.
Dickens too, in his smaller way, can persuade his readers that
a character like Micawber, based on a purely artificial formula,
is really a flesh and blood creature abounding in life.

Giotto never failed to produce this effect, not only in his
individual figures but in his groups of figures (see Fig. 1). With
the period-vision at his disposal, and notwithstanding the new
material he added to it, he could not possibly have the grasp
of the visual world that came so easily to a Tintoretto or a
Rembrandt. Yet in spite of these limitations one can walk all
round his figures, one can gauge their distance from the eye,
feel their weight on the ground, sense the solidity of the limbs
under the draperies. Nor does this apply only to his figures.
Their settings too have the same reality. The hills, trees, houses,
meadows among which they find themselves are as convincing
as they are themselves.

When one adds to this Shakespearean *completeness* which
makes everything credible, a Shakespearean *profundity* which
makes everything deeply moving, one can take something of the
measure of this extraordinary painter. I have no need to apologize
for devoting so much space to him. He sowed so many and such
various seeds that there is hardly any aspect of art during the
next few centuries that is not traceable to him, and though in
any given direction he was destined to be outstripped by later
men, no other painter ever held so many trump cards at once.
Fra Angelico developed his sweetness, Raphael his balance,
Michelangelo his sense of gesture, Piero his sense of space,
Masaccio his sense of drama, many later painters made use of
his feeling for landscape, but in none of them were all these gifts
combined. To study the frescoes in the Arena chapel at Padua

is to realize that a new era in art has been born capable of growth in any number of different directions; that here is the starting point for a new set of adventures and that Giotto provided signposts for them all.

As though bewildered by the possibilities suddenly opened up to it, Florentine painting produced only two important men during the century following Giotto's death. Fra Angelico was in spirit a late Gothic miniature painter. Born in France or England he would perhaps have decorated a few illuminated manuscripts that would have been among the loveliest of their kind. But he was a Florentine by birth and he was carried along on the Florentine current and given opportunities which no French or English monastery would have provided. He rose to them magnificently, as long as he was not asked to be solemn or profound. He managed somehow to convert the patterned sweetness that was one half of Gothic and raise it to a higher power. One is so much tempted to think of him always as a master of pure pale colour and smooth untroubled line that it often comes as a slight shock to find how capable he is of nobility and even sturdiness in designing the general framework of his big compositions. His *naïveté* is a *naïveté* of detail, not of general conception. From Giotto he learned the value of simplicity, but it was left to Masaccio to exploit Giotto's sense of drama and to develop his sense of structure and solidity. If Giotto had created a set of signposts it was Masaccio who chose the most important of them and managed to follow the road along which it led for a surprising distance before his death at the age of twenty-seven. By this time (1428) Florentine tradition had begun to crystallize. During the century that followed the death of Giotto it was always possible that Giotto might prove to be an isolated figure, a giant without progeny. But after the death of Masaccio the course of Florentine painting was assured. It continued in an astonishing crescendo for just over a century and then ceased almost as suddenly as it had begun.

Before examining what that century brought forth it will be as well to go back to the century that elapsed between Giotto and Masaccio and note that however barren it may have been in Florence it was by no means barren in Siena. Indeed there were moments during the course of that century when it looked as though Siena and not Florence was going to decide the future of European painting.

It would be silly to exaggerate the difference in spirit between the two cities. Historians of art have been tempted to say that

Florence looked forward to the coming Renaissance while Siena remained mediæval at heart. There is a grain of truth in the over-statement, but Fra Angelico was certainly mediæval at heart and yet no one could mistake Fra Angelico for a Sienese. The two cities are different and their art is different, but the difference is not so much between two conceptions of life as between two conceptions of art. There is more than a suspicion of "art for art's sake" in Sienese painting. In Giotto and Masaccio there is none. In the struggle between truth and beauty which underlies all art, beauty is inclined to get the upper hand in Siena, truth in Florence. Duccio (1255–1319) is almost as wholeheartedly a narrative painter as Giotto, but whenever his narrative seems to be leading him into harshness or angularity he will abandon it. And if that is true of Duccio it is truer still of Simone Martini (see Fig. 4), whose sense of colour is so exquisite that nothing would induce him to subordinate it to the mood of his narrative. If Siena clings to the Byzantine tradition it is not through conservatism but through intellectual laziness. What the Sienese have to express has nothing to do with Byzantium, but here is a serviceable set of idioms to hand, so why not use them? Nothing in the Sienese spirit has made them obsolete. Florence throws them overboard without hesitation or regret, Siena adapts them to her needs. Occasionally a particularly intense emotional conception, like the angel seated on the tomb in Duccio's panel of the "Three Marys," or the shrinking Madonna in Simone's "Annunciation," seems to demand a new set of shapes, a complete departure from tradition. Giotto would have gone straight to nature in such cases. Duccio and Simone did not. They produced the new shapes by a sheer effort of invention. They had a sense of rhythm which could, when necessary, dispense with a sense of actuality. When that sense failed them the result was mere affectation. When it did not they reach imaginative heights attained by no other school of painting.

As for the kind of life depicted in their narrative painting it is an altogether more delicate, aristocratic affair than in Florence. The Sienese seem to have richer furniture in their houses, finer needlework on their brocaded dresses, gayer patterns on their tiled floors, Lorenzetti's "Nativity of the Virgin" in Siena gives the impression of a family that had spared no expense when setting up house, still more so Sassetta's picture of the same subject at Asciano. But the Sienese school had none of the stamina of Florence. It could see life in the round, but it could not set that life firmly on the earth's surface. Sienese figures may be round but they are not solid. They are no longer cardboard like Byzantine figures: they have the three-dimensional existence of a balloon but not the weight of a boulder. Sassetta, the last of the great Sienese painters, could paint the betrothal of St. Francis to his three mystical maidens, who immediately and without giving the spectator the faintest spasm of surprise, float gaily away through the air. If Giotto had tackled the subject one would unconsciously look for the mechanism that enabled them to perform this charming act of levitation. In the end the robuster art of Florence was bound to win. After Sassetta, Sienese art ceased to have a character of its own. It enjoyed its moment of exquisiteness and then succumbed to Florence.

I do not propose to follow the course of Florentine art during the one hundred and three years between the death of Masaccio and that of Michelangelo in detail. The list of considerable artists, both painters and sculptors, is a long one—longer than in any other period of the same duration. Each of them has his own particular kind of excitement to spur him on, and all of them give the same exhilarating sense of being proud to be in a movement, to be caught up by it and to contribute to it.

The Renaissance in Italy meant two things in particular. It meant first of all the rediscovery of Greece and Rome, and that in its turn meant not merely the digging up of a few Græco-Roman statues and the discovering of a few Greek and Roman writings. It meant the realization that civilization was a continuous thing stretching back into the past and therefore to be visualized as stretching forward with magnificent possibilities into the future. It gave the Florentines a sense of belonging to history, and of being both competitors and spiritual descendants of the Athenians. Secondly, the Renaissance meant freedom of mind, freedom to gratify curiosity about everything under the sun: freedom to question everything old and to invent anything new. It meant the habit of asking "Why?" and "How?" and the consequent question so admirably condensed by America, "So what?"

In a word the two qualities which gave the Italian Renaissance its distinctive flavour were a passionate desire for knowledge and a passionate belief in experiment, especially the kind of experiment that puts knowledge to the test. And it was the special gift of Florence to be able to combine the two in her art.

Knowledge by itself can easily lead to pedantry: experiment

by itself to mere novelty. The Florentines balanced the two and escaped both pitfalls. They had the wisdom to use both as means and not as ends. If you had asked any of them "as means to what end?" they would probably have found it difficult to give a neat answer, but to-day with our bird's-eye view of the massive accomplishment of the Italian Renaissance (the hundred best years of Florence, from 1430 to 1530, plus the hundred and forty best of Venice, say, 1440 to 1590), we can answer, "To an expression of the fullness of life." It is one of those grandiose phrases from which an Englishman instinctively shrinks, but the spirit that produced the Colleoni statue, the Dresden Madonna, the Sacristy of San Lorenzo and the Last Supper is too big to take English self-consciousness into account.   It requires grandiose phrases.

Two factors which made for continuity of tradition during the High Renaissance must be mentioned. One was the Bottega system whereby each well-known artist in fifteenth-century Florence had his own studio with apprentices as young as ten or twelve years of age who learned the whole business of picture-making from grinding colours, preparing grounds and transferring cartoons to painting portions of the master's pictures. The other was the general level of enlightenment among patrons, who managed, with a minimum of interference, to stimulate artistic production to a remarkable degree, both in quantity and quality. It would be roughly true to say that while the artists themselves were enlarging their means through technical and semi-scientific research, patrons were spurring them on to use these means to new and exciting ends.

The most useful way, for once, to cover the period will be the conventional one of picking out a few major figures and describing their personal contribution to the art of the century. And the easiest way to visualise its developments is to picture it as a river system in which many tributaries are drawn gradually together until their separate waters mix in the achievements of Michelangelo, Raphael and Leonardo.

Paolo Uccello (1397–1475) has achieved fame as the man who worked out and applied to his pictures the principles of perspective. One almost wishes he had not done so. In his sense of decoration he is almost Oriental. In his affectionate love of detail and incident he is Gothic. His rather absurd insistence on vanishing points does perhaps help him to *organize* his painting in depth, but I cannot feel that his painting of the "Rout of San Romano" in the National Gallery was ever *conceived* in depth.

It is surely strange that the man who made possible the change from the panel-on-the-wall to the window-cut-in-the-wall belonged so wholeheartedly to the first, though his chief recorded contribution to the science of painting was in the direction of the second.

Piero della Francesa (1416–1492) also had a scientific and intellectual approach to painting which has very little connection with his genius as an artist. In his "Nativity" at the National Gallery one's first and lasting impression is of a hushed serenity. It is as though for the first time an artist had managed to paint silence. Action is suspended. The ashen blues and greys, the smooth surfaces, the untroubled, expressionless faces of the Madonna and the angels, the acutely sensitive line that never flows, never hurries and yet never ceases to move, all add to the mood that Piero made his own. He is the most restrained, the least dramatic and the least romantic of all Florentine painters, but in many ways the profoundest. At the present moment fashionable taste, following an instinct for purity, has transferred its allegiance from Botticelli to Piero. Fashionable taste, which is always to be suspected, but never to be despised, sees in Piero's science and in the intense seriousness with which he worked out the spatial relationships (especially those that lead *into* the picture) between the component parts of his picture, a firmer basis for painting than the lyrical exquisiteness of Botticelli (1447–1510), to whom the scientific research side of the Renaissance made no appeal at all. The humanity of Giotto, the solidity of Masaccio, the deep space of Piero failed to interest Botticelli. In his lack of grasp of the three-dimensional world Botticelli dated back to the time of Fra Angelico, but in his power over his own two-dimensional world he has never been surpassed. If the quality of his vision was archaistic, his way of translating it into paint was far more sophisticated than that of any of his contemporaries. The modulated arabesque of his line is astonishing, the subtlety with which it turns this way and that, always suggesting movement and never relaxing its tension. No less subtle is his sense of pattern. Like Uccello, Botticelli was a decorator, but unlike most decorators, he used his gifts to express an intensely personal mood. It is not an easy mood to describe, for it somehow combines languor with litheness, voluptuousness with purity, the warmth of a summer evening with the cold tang of a spring dawn. In the "Birth of Venus" and "Primavera," both painted as decorations for the villa of Lorenzo and Giovanni de' Medici, this fusion of innocence and

sophistication is extraordinary. Botticelli could "quote" the
Roman Medici Venus almost line for line in his painting of the
nude goddess, and yet turn her into a Madonna as virginal as
Duccio's. Botticelli may not have been an innovator in the
science of picture-making, but in giving a Christian twist to the
pagan world he bestowed upon the word "Renaissance" a richer
meaning.

Antonio Pollaiuolo was as interested in the nude as Botticelli,
but for different reasons. His was the inquiring scientific spirit
of Piero, but not being a poet it was with difficulty that he avoided
the pitfall of pedantry. Anatomy was his particular passion and
he set himself deliberately to tackle one of the most difficult of
all painters' problems, the representation of the naked male in
action. He succeeded admirably, and in doing so considerably
enlarged the field of painting for all his successors. His pictures,
however, are not lovable or attractive, for though they have a
splendid vigour they always give the sense of being little more
than masterly essays in violent movement. In his "Martyrdom of
San Sebastian" (National Gallery), for example (see Fig. 15),
the group of archers display their muscles rather like a troupe of
acrobats or wrestlers. They would hardly be disturbed, one feels,
if the Saint were removed and an archer's target substituted.

The reputation of Verocchio (1435–1488) rests partly on his
having had the most important workshop in Florence during the
third quarter of the Fifteenth Century, partly on his statue of the
Venetian Condottiere Bartolomeo Colleoni, and partly on his
impeccable craftsmanship. The Colleoni statue is one of those
isolated achievements, like Gray's "Elegy," in which an artist
sometimes manages to rise well above his own normal level. In
conception it contains nothing new—the proudly stepping horse
carrying the conventionally haughty gangster—but it is perfect
of its kind and no other equestrian statue I have seen has such
an immediate appeal. But it is Verocchio's position in the
development of Florentine art that is significant. Without con-
tributing much to it he stands, as it were, at the junction of all
the pioneer tributaries and prepares the way for his pupil
Leonardo. Verocchio has, in a mild degree, the qualities of so
many of his predecessors that it is not easy to distinguish his own
personal quality. It is only by noting what Leonardo got out of
him that one begins to see what he had in him.

Leonardo himself (1452–1519) is too good to be true. He seems
more like the creation of a romantic historical nobelist than a
human being. He sums up the spirit of the High Renaissance

almost too completely. The Leonardo legend is too well known to need elaboration here. The endless inquisitiveness, the ceaseless experiment, the torrent of creative ideas, so few of which came to maturity, the incredible energy that always seemed on the point of achieving so much, but left so little behind, and yet stamped that little with an unforgettable flavour—all this is excellent material for legend. What is so strange in him is the mixture between relentless scientific curiosity on the one hand and mystical romanticism on the other. The combination seems unnatural. It is as though one were to admire the Parthenon for its classic severity of line and proportion, and then, on entering it, find it filled with the glowing Gothic mystery of thirteenth-century stained glass. If Leonardo's life were not so completely documented, I have no doubt that theorists would have attempted to prove that he was not one person but two, and that the hand that painted the Gioconda was not the same that wrote the Note-books.

However, it is with Leonardo, the painter and sculptor, that this book is concerned, and though from his paintings one can guess at a massive intellect one could hardly deduce the empirical scientist and inventor. In an earlier chapter I have already spoken of the "Last Supper" and of how it marked a climax in picture construction. It is the supreme example of the "classic" side of high Renaissance art, just as the "Virgin of the Rocks" and the "Gioconda" represent its romantic side. But as a painter Leonardo is less typical of his time than Raphael (1483–1520). Every one of Leonardo's major works seems to be a concentrated effort, a frontal attack launched for the purposes of exploring a chosen set of possibilities. Raphael was not an explorer. His gift lay in following the pioneers, in taking advantage of the ground they had prepared and in consolidating it. He could take hints thrown out by lesser artists and give them a new meaning: or absorb the spirit of the only two men who could dwarf him (Leonardo and Michelangelo) and incorporate it into his own work without becoming too apparent a plagiarist (see Fig. 5). He had neither the intellect of Leonardo nor the dynamism of Michelangelo. In fact any attempt to explain what Raphael contributed to the sum of Florentine painting is sure to sound unconvincing because whichever of his qualities one selects as typical of him, one can always think of some other Florentine painter who possessed the same qualities to a greater degree. His sweetness? But Perugino, his master, was even sweeter. His power to organize a big composition? But Leonardo had even higher powers of organization. His sense of balance? But it was no greater then Piero's. His power to invent rhetorical gesture? But there he was a weak imitator of Michelangelo. Any cold-blooded analysis of Raphael is bound to see him as an eclectic. Perhaps he was; if so he is the only eclectic who deserves to be ranked as a genius. He carried the science of picture construction, the capacity for pure design to such a pitch of perfection that, for once, perfection seems to take the place of imagination. His Dresden Madonna is in essence a mere amalgam of elements invented by Perugino and Michelangelo, yet the poise and balance of the figure is so subtle, so suave, and so inevitable that one forgets that it is built up of second-hand parts.

What Michelangelo (1475–1564) stood for has already been implied. There is a rare type of artist on whom the very laws of art seem to impose intolerable restrictions—who always seems to be endeavouring to express something more than his medium is capable of expressing. Such men do not occur often. One's admiration of them is always mingled with a slight sense of discomfort. When Bethoven manages to condense into his late quartettes something that is beyond even the capacity of a full orchestra it seems as if the boundaries of music itself were being overstepped. Not because Beethoven fails as a musician, but because music is too small a thing to contain him. The means at his disposal are inadequate for the end in view. In the same way Shakespeare's emotional pressure does, at times, strain the capacity of language to breaking point. For Michelangelo neither marble nor paint was quite adequate for his needs. Among painters he is the exact opposite of, say, Velasquez, whose greatness depends on his recognition of the capacity of paint and his wizardry in handling it.

Michelangelo was a passionate specialist, interested like Pollaiuolo exclusively in the male human body. Like Beethoven, who chose to make four-stringed instruments the vehicle of his profoundest inventions, Michelangelo chose to make the human body express everything he had to say. His figures inhabit no planet. Such references to landscape as his narrative compels him to make, like the tree in the Garden of Eden, are mere stage properties. The race of men he created resides in the bleak mountains of the moon. No particular quality of light falls on them, no air surrounds them. They have no environment. They exist in their own right. Michelangelo began where Pollaiuolo left off. Or rather Michelangelo used the human body as an empty vessel to pour himself into, whereas to Pollaiuolo it was a piece of machinery interesting only as an admirable example of engineering.

For all its complex architectural cohesion the Sistine Chapel ceiling, which Michelangelo completed in 1512, is essentially a collection of significant single figures or pairs of figures. The thirteen men in Leonardo's Last Supper are bound together by a continuous thread of drama and design: each is inseparable from its neighbour. Not so the Sistine Chapel figures. Each one is a self-contained invention with a gesture and a mood of its own. If the gesture is more rhetorical than in any previous Renaissance painting, the mood is always intense enough to justify the rhetoric and even to make it inevitable.

But despite the Sistine Chapel Michelangelo was at heart not a painter, but a sculptor. In fact, each one of the Sistine Chapel athletes, Sibyls and Prophets is a statue *manqué*. What has been said of his painting is even more true of his carving. The four figures that flank the seated statues of Lorenzo and Giuliano de Medici in the Sacristy of San Lorenzo are enough to judge him by. They are not merely human bodies in effectively semi-recumbent poses, as they would have been had they been carved by an Athenian of the Periclean age. They are expressionist interpretations of Day and Night, Dawn and Dusk. A modern sculptor would tackle the same problem by abandoning ana-tomical accuracy (see Figs. 31 and 32). Michelangelo's surprising achievement is to have drawn upon a profound knowledge of anatomy and turned it to expressionist purposes.

One important name has been omitted from my list of picked Florentines. Verocchio provided Leonardo with a spring-board, but Donatello (1386–1466) was too great a man to be a mere spring-board even for Michelangelo. Sculpture in Northern Italy had not run the steady course that is traceable in painting. It progressed rather in a series of disconnected outbursts, which is all the more curious when one remembers how vivid a stimulus was given to the Renaissance by Græco-Roman sculpture. True, the earliest of the North Italian sculptors, Nicola Pisano and his son Giovanni, abound in Roman mannerisms, but Ghiberti and Donatello were anything but slavish disciples of what we now think of as the Classical spirit in sculpture. Ghiberti had a strong feeling for the picturesque and Donatello a sense of character that goes far beyond the merely physical. His Saint George is the slim, eager young undergraduate not only in type, but in poise, in the sensitiveness of his finger-tips resting on his shield, in the suggestion of standing on tiptoe: his statue of Zuccone verges on caricature in its shrinking ungainly pose as well as in its strongly marked features. It was this subtle sense of gesture that Michelangelo seized on and turned to his own uses, though he never possessed—or never felt the need of— Donatello's psychological insight.

There are moments in the development of art when the air is full of promise and each new achievement seems like a stepping stone to desirable but unattainable ends. Such a period was in-augurated by Masaccio. There are other moments in which the end has suddenly been reached and the way to further progress is barred. Raphael, Leonardo and Michelangelo between them produced such an *impasse* in Florence. The perfection of Raphael could not be further perfected, though Fra Bartolommeo made an attempt to do so and Andrea del Sarto half-heartedly tried to add to Raphael's suavity a note of drama. The intellectual side of Leonardo was inimitable, but his romantic side could be reduced to a formula. Leonardo's rockbound, subaqueous gloom and particularly the famous faraway smile became mannerisms that certain Milanese artists adopted only to find that they led nowhere. Michelangelo was even more obstructive to develop-ment. Rhetoric is the most dangerous of all modes of expression; only passionate sincerity can justify it. Without sincerity it becomes a mere bundle of easily imitated mannerisms. Michel-angelo's imitators were a set of dwarfish thieves who recklessly borrowed his giant's robe, and collapsed under its weight. Florentine painting ended suddenly in meaningless posturings, after a hundred of the most creative years that art has ever known.

But while Florentine art was exhausting itself by the very splendour of its own achievement, the Venetians were exploring a new set of pictorial possibilities. At those moments when development pauses because possibilities seem to have been ex-hausted in a given direction the new impetus usually comes through what a mathematician would call an enlargement of the bracket. The idea contained in the formula, $a+b$, is not quite the same as that contained in $(a+b)$. It has already been seen that the Egyptian formula for "head" was "eye plus pro-file," and that there was no valid reason against combining the front view of an eye with a side view of a face. The Egyptian had not put a bracket around the eye-plus-profile formula. In the same way the Florentines, who had pushed the science of picture organization to its fullest limits, had not yet arrived at the stage of bracketing that science with the science of colour. This is what the Venetians did, and by doing so opened up a new set of possibilities. To a Florentine of 1480 a picture was composed of shape plus colour; to a Venetian of 1520 it was shape fused with colour. To the Florentine, colour, however harmonious, was a quality to be *added* to design. To the Venetian it was inseparable from design. To the Florentine it was an attribute of the object to which it belonged: a red dress or a green tree were patches of red and green confined within the boundaries of those objects. The Venetians thought of colour as a quality without which the dress or the tree could hardly be said to exist. It permeated everything and flowed across contours like light: it caressed each object like air. The structural unity of Florentine painting gave place to the chromatic unity of Venetian. It is not by accident that the best period of Venetian art produced no great sculptors.

It is in the paintings of Giovanni Bellini (1430–1516) that this new quality is first seen. Bellini began by being dominated by the steely asceticism of Mantegna, and he moved slowly towards the point where light and colour become paramount ingredients in his art. Giorgione and Titian seized on the new discovery, gradually relaxing their linear tension and their structural sense, and replacing them by a set of glowing harmonies that had their origin in light rather than colour. Florentine colour had never been timid; it was, at its best, as intense as anything the Venetians could achieve, but it did not radiate or burn. Titian's colour is often almost subdued, Tintoretto's gloomy, Veronese's muffled, but Titian's greys and dull purples have more fire in them than Fra Angelico's vermilions and pale ultramarines. In fact Titian set his foot on the road that led directly to nineteenth-century impressionism in that he did not paint the thing-as-he-knew-it, but the thing-as-he-saw-it. A green hillside can be purple if it is in the shadow, a brown field scarlet if it is seen at sunset. Titian did not push his researches anything like as far as the French impressionists, but in all his paintings there is a sensuous pervasion of light that ties all the parts together in a closer relationship than they ever had before, and in particular binds the figures and the landscape into a single harmony.

Landscape had not yet reached the point where it could exist in its own right without the justification of figures, but Venetian landscape fused itself intimately with the figures, whereas in Florentine painting it was seldom more than a theatre backcloth.

The extreme example of this Venetian fusion is Giorgione's "Tempest," that enigmatic masterpiece which can be classified neither as a landscape in which the foreground figures are disturbingly important nor as a figure painting in which the landscape plays an unusually dominant part. It is in this picture that one first notices a new method of composition which was later to become the landscape painter's favourite system. The normal Florentine painting is based on the pyramid, the picture piled up more or less symmetrically round a central mass. Giorgione's picture has no central mass: on the contrary, its centre is a gap through which the eye is invited to pass in order to penetrate into the furthest recesses of the landscape.

A change of mood runs parallel to the change of method. A languor creeps in and an opulence that bears witness to a more worldly view of life. In Giorgione's "Fête Champêtre" the young men and maidens are no longer alert and eager-eyed. They are creatures of leisure enjoying the summer afternoon; and though this, again, is an extreme case, the same glowing languor runs through much of the later work of Giovanni Bellini, the whole of Giorgione, and a high percentage of Titian.

It is difficult to write of Giorgione and Titian in a way that will give an idea of their stature as compared with the other great artists of Europe. One cannot write of Giotto without calling him a giant: he saw and painted so much that had never been so painted before. Nor of Michelangelo: his field of expression was narrow, but the intensity of his expression was breathtaking. But Giorgione and Titian were not great innovators like Giotto, nor had they the rather frightening power of Michelangelo. Yet they, too, were giants, but giants who are not to be described by strong words or superlatives. Giorgione's quality was the indefinable one of aristocracy—and though the word itself is derived from a Greek superlative meaning simply "best," our sense to-day of what it means is narrowed and dimmed. Giorgione was one of the tragic young men of art, like Schubert and Keats, who died young because the gods hate anti-climax. Giorgione would certainly have developed had he lived, but he could never in later life have created anything that so perfectly combined worldliness with purity. In his painting he seems to embrace pleasure fearlessly, and yet it is pleasure purged of every trace of grossness. Titian had not the same aristocracy, but his stature was greater still. He lived to be an old man, and his vast output is uneven in quality, but the best of it is stamped not by aristocracy, but by nobility. There is less refinement but more big-heartedness in it than in Giorgione's. As he grew older his knowledge of the play of light grew more and more profound; he saw his world less and less in terms of contour and more and more in terms of shimmering surface, and his style grew broader and more impressionist. His imagination was seldom of a very high order. It is only rarely that he can bring one face to face with the tense moment when all emotional threads seem to be tied together. He did achieve it once or twice, as in the "Entombment" in the Louvre, but such pictures are exceptional. It is the whole glowing corpus of his work that counts, not the isolated masterpiece.

Tintoretto (1518–1594) carried Venetian painting a stage further. He, too, produced an occasional painting that etches itself permanently in the memory like the "Bacchus and Ariadne" in the ante-collegio of the Ducal Palace in Venice, but he is like Titian in that one remembers his general flavour rather than particular instances of it. More dynamic than Titian, his paintings seem to be a flicker with a dark blue flame. Serenity is gone and a kind of troubled ecstasy takes its place.

In Chapter IV I attempted to describe the meaning of "baroque"—that enlargement of the bracket to include the whole of visual experience which occurred about the beginning of the Seventeenth Century. In Tintoretto one is getting very near to it. Far more than Titian he is a link between the Classic and the Baroque age. In him both light and colour are almost independent of structure. Tintoretto will boldly throw a whole group of figures into deep shadow, or allow the light to pick out and isolate a hand or knee. His composition no longer follows the contours, but builds itself up in masses of tone and colour. He breaks away from the Renaissance system of symmetry and frontality and permits himself to paint a Crucifixion from the side or to visualise a Last Supper in which the table is seen in diagonal perspective.

With Veronese the imaginative temperature begins to drop. Giorgione's aristocracy, Titian's warmth, Tintoretto's drama are toned down into pageantry. True, Veronese's pageantry is of a high order, but Venetian worldliness has by this time gained the upper hand. The satins and brocades that gave Titian an excuse for showing his mastery of the caressing veil of light are now a mere opportunity for expensive display. Not that there is any trace of vulgarity in his painting, but that his eye is caught and held by opulence and cannot penetrate beyond it. Veronese was a prince of decorators. After him came a long lull. Italy ceased to be the focus of European painting, but there are one or two isolated outbursts of energy that must be noted before taking up the story elsewhere. In Venice herself, long after the main creative current had become sluggish, Tiepolo (1696–1770) gave it a momentary new activity by his ceiling paintings. If pageantry was the keynote of Veronese, swagger was that of Tiepolo. There is an airy stylishness in all his work. He inherited and exploited all the baroque mannerisms, including the conception of a ceiling as a hole punched in the roof through which could be seen a sky filled with flying and floating creatures, and the wild rhetoric of gesture for gesture's sake. But Tiepolo's sense of design and his elegant, rather acid colour saved him from emptiness.

So ends the succession of giants in Venetian painting. It would be as futile to discuss whether Venice or Florence produced the greater masterpieces as to discuss whether reason or instinct is the more potent arbiter in human affairs. One factor—a technical one—makes Venetian art seem closer to our own than Florentine, namely, the change over from tempera to oil as the normal medium for paint. Love of surfaces as opposed to love of contour was doubtless a Venetian characteristic, and the oil medium encouraged the development of that side of the artist's vision. Perhaps Florence would have rejected oil painting as unsuitable to her needs, or perhaps she would have adopted it but ignored its possibilities, or perhaps, had it been adopted earlier, it would have revolutionized Florentine painting. Such speculations are vain. The two schools are distinct both in outlook and in technique. But there was another deciding factor in the difference between the two cities. Florence never had the same kind of civic pride as Venice. She was an art-producing centre, and as such supplied the needs of the Church and to a lesser extent of the noble families. Venice, on the other hand, was a city of merchants and palaces and great civic buildings, and the artists of Venice were called upon to serve the city as much as the church. The palace of the Doges contain some of the major examples of Venetian painting, and the theme of most of them was Venice herself. Veronese put all he knew into the great oval "Apotheosis of Venice," but even his huge pseudo-religious paintings—the "Feast in the House of Levi," for example—are really tributes to the extravagantly colourful texture of Venetian life. There was nothing in Florence to correspond to this aspect of civic pride—no parallel, for instance, to the ceremony in which the Doge celebrated the marriage of Venice to the Adriatic by throwing a ring into the sea from the state barge, the *Bucentaur*, that appears in so many Venetian paintings.

There was a third factor in determining the distinctive flavour of Venetian art. Venice looked Eastwards; her trade was with the Near East. Constantinople supplied her with some delicious material loot, but the loot was not entirely material. Venetian taste had an Oriental tinge. The city that could erect the half-Oriental Basilica of St. Mark, pale and glittering like an opal, was bound to develop a very different kind of painting from the city that approved of the stern proportions of young Brunelleschi's dome in Florence.

Two other Italians must be mentioned: Correggio (1489–1534), who worked in isolation in Parma, and more than any other artist helped to establish the baroque formula long before it passed into general currency; and Caravaggio (1499–1530), who threw overboard all the aristocratic traditions of Italian painting and stressed the earthly rather than the worldly, and made it more emphatic by painting it in a hard, chilly light with deep black shadows that gave him and his school the title "chiaroscurists." Caravaggio would not be of the least importance in the history of painting were it not that his influence spread to Spain by way of Naples and that the young Velasquez, temporarily fascinated by it, proved that even a superficial outlook in the hands of a master may sometimes produce a great work of art.

CHAPTER X

FLANDERS, GERMANY, SPAIN, HOLLAND

TINTORETTO and Veronese were not only the last of the great Venetians. They were the last of the great Italians. Once they had ceased to paint, Italy was no longer the artistic centre of Europe. The stream and its tributaries, clearly defined so far, now becomes difficult to follow. A Cretan, Domenicos Theotocopulos, trained in Venice, went unaccountably to Spain, and there painted pictures so strangely moving that he is still the most disturbingly personal of all painters. A Fleming, Peter Paul Rubens, journeyed to Italy, soaked himself in Michelangelo and Titian, returned to Antwerp, established a kind of picture factory and poured out a series of pictures of astonishing vitality. Thus were the seeds of seventeenth-century painting planted in Spain and Flanders. The main Italian stream, instead of adding new tributaries to itself, split into two.

Domenicos Theotocopulos, commonly known as el Greco, is the first notable name in Spanish painting, but Rubens's name is by no means the first in Flanders. From about 1400 onwards Flemish painting had been pursuing a quiet course of its own parallel to but only dimly- dependent on the course of Italian painting. For a combination of complicated political reasons (comparative peacefulness, the protection of the Dukes of Burgundy and flourishing trade were among the most important of them), it happened that the Lowlands at the beginning of the Fifteenth Century were in a much more favourable position than France to foster the arts. The spirit of the Renaissance as it manifested itself in Italy hardly touched Northern Europe. There were none of the new and intoxicating impulses that were in the Florentine air. Nevertheless, something was in the air. Part of the Gothic spirit was dead, but part of it remained and vitalized the early Flemish painters. The superstition, the childish delight in whimsy, the grotesque side of the Gothic spirit had sobered down, but the intense curiosity about things in general remained. Consequently the Flemish painters who were contemporary with Masaccio and Piero had none of their nobility or serenity, but an abundance of vitality and an avidity for detail that is astonishing. Jan van Eyck, the earliest of them, perfected the use of the oil medium, though he had no idea of its possibilities or of the effect it was to have on the course of European painting. It gave his painting depth and brilliance, but he went on painting as the masters of tempera had painted, clinging to the contour, thinking in terms of line. No Italian painter gives the same impression of snatching greedily at the charmingly intricate spectacle of life as van Eyck, or Rogier van der Weyden, or Memlinc or Pieter Breughel (the last and greatest member of this subsidiary Renaissance). Their pictures have this common characteristic that they are never tired of *describing* what they see. "Johannes de Eyck fuit hic" is inscribed on the portrait of Arnolfini and his wife—just as a descriptive reporter's article might be headed "by an Eye Witness." The two words perfectly describe the whole school. They are witnesses whose veracity no one would dream of doubting because they have sworn themselves in to paint the whole visual truth and nothing but the visual truth. Arnolfini's circular mirror, his shoes, his hat, his furniture must have been just like that. Van Eyck "was there." The great Van Eyck altarpiece, the "Adoration of the Lamb" at Ghent, has no parallel in Italy. Despite its mystical implications it has no mystery. It is no more than a highly organized inventory of earthly experiences seen through the eyes of an acute and sensitive observer who knew what was meant by reverence but was unaware of the existence of ecstasy. Memlinc was more prosaic, van der Weyden more subtle, Pieter Breughel more humorous and much more interested in action. But all of them are eye witnesses with voracious, unjaded eyes. I hate to dismiss them so briefly, especially Pieter Breughel, who is unique among painters, and whose painting never fails to produce in me a special thrill. He seems to me to get more of the quality of affection into his paintings than any other artist. In his case the word "affection" has connotations which need qualifying by the addition of the word "gusto." He is rollicking, but never flamboyant. He is crisp, but never dry. He gives his evidence with an unswerving respect for truth: he is always on oath. But he gives it with bucolic relish. It is the *happening* that excites him, the peasant sweating in the cornfield, dancing in the village street, swallowing good food at table (see Fig. 16), skating on the frozen pond. The only other painter I can think of who can give the same impression of delighting (and communicating delight) in the quaintness of human activity is the modern British painter, Stanley Spencer. With both artists Gothic fervour seems to have detached itself from religion and attached itself to life, especially village life.

Meanwhile in Germany the struggle between the native Gothic and the spreading influence of the Renaissance was producing rather a different atmosphere. It is noteworthy that each part of North-Western Europe resisted the Renaissance in its own way—resisted it until it became too strong to be kept at bay any longer. In every country except Italy the Gothic spirit died hard, and the Renaissance, when it did come, came fully fledged. Renaissance mannerisms were common enough among the fifteenth-century Flemish painters, but they were no more than mannerisms. The whole school provided, in fact, a kind of Gothic swan song with Pieter Breughel as its final climax. Rubens, born eight years after Breughel's death, brought to Flanders an entirely new set of values—Baroque at its most exuberant. There is no one to bridge the gap between Breughel and Rubens.

In Germany there was no such gap, partly because there the Gothic swan song (performed by Grünewald) was more sophisticated than Breughel's, partly because the only artist outside

Italy who managed to absorb more than the superficial aspects of the Renaissance point of view was a German. Dürer (1471–1528) had much of Leonardo's scientific and intellectual equipment. On to his harsh native German realism he grafted something of Italian scholarship. His famous "Melancolia" engraving is a strange mixture of the new science and the old superstition. Dürer was not a born painter, but he lifted the art of engraving on metal and wood on to a higher plane. Like the Flemish artists, he had none of the Italian grace, but, unlike them, he tried hard to catch at some of the Italian nobility; he visited Venice, watched the aged Giovanni Bellini at work and envied him his power to render the glow and serenity of nature, but his own natural ruggedness and honesty would not permit him to copy what he could not genuinely absorb. In most of Dürer's work one feels the mediæval world is not far below the surface, though it rarely breaks through.

But the typical German painter was Grünewald, who summed up everything he had to say, and what is more, gave complete expression to the German spirit, in his great altarpiece now at Colmar. There is nothing at all like it in the whole history of art. Tortured almost to the point of hysteria, grotesque yet sublime, it has the curious effect of looking back to the Gothic artists and forward to the Baroque masters at the same time. It is an uncomfortable but deeply moving work. The detail shown in Fig. 2 gives something of Grünewald's quality. One has only to compare it with the detail from Giotto's "Lamentation" at Padua (Fig. 1) to realize the profound difference in temper between Germany and Italy.

A generation later, Hans Holbein worked in Basle but was tempted to England by the prospect of portrait painting under Henry VIII. It is not easy to define what it is in Holbein's portraits that makes them memorable, but one realizes their quiet strength as soon as one compares them with those of his French contemporary, Jean Clouet. Clouet's draughtsmanship, more delicate and refined than Holbein's, is too elegant to be quite honest. Holbein's portraits always seem to be focusing one's attention, quietly but insistently, on the subtle shades of difference between his sitter of the moment and the rest of mankind. Psychologically they do not penetrate very deep: one cannot hear his sitters' voices or imagine their smiles as one can with the portraits of Rembrandt or Goya. But Holbein could grasp and express the structure of a man's skull, the texture of skin, the fleshiness of a cheek by the slightest inflexions of his pencil or brush. One is reminded of those rare actors on the stage who make their points without either raising or lowering their voices. In his restraint and integrity Holbein was not typically German. What stamps him as a German is his robustness and his tendency to stress the character of his sitter by coarsening rather than refining his features.

With the death of Breughel the last traces of medievalism disappeared and Europe as a whole was ready to accept the new discoveries that came to fruition in the Seventeenth Century. Italy made those discoveries and then, as it were, lost interest in them. It was perhaps by chance that El Greco introduced them to Spain, or that they took such firm root there, but it was almost inevitable that they should find a foothold in Flanders and Holland. The Church had for long been almost the sole employer of the painter though Venice had begun to break the monopoly by using him for civic propaganda. But a new force was growing up. Even in Venice the rich merchant was beginning to make himself felt as a power, and with the shifting westwards of the commercial centre of gravity in Europe, the artistic centre of gravity shifted too. It was almost inevitable that Flanders and Holland should become for a time the art centres of Europe and that the stimulus to production should pass more and more into the hands of the merchant princes.

Especially was this inevitable in Protestant Holland. In Catholic Flanders the Church still retained her position as the artist's most reliable employer.

To Rubens, however, it hardly mattered who employed him. If the Church wanted a Crucifixion or an Assumption (see Fig. 22) he would paint a dashing but hardly a moving one, for though he was a good Catholic he was no mystic. If a princely patron wanted a "Toilet of Venus" or a "Bath of Diana" or a "Nymphs surprised by Satyrs" he would set about it with equal vigour, crowding the canvas with an exuberant mass of forms which in the hands of any other painter would have been chaotic. Rubens was afraid of nothing, had no limitations except the serious one of having both feet firmly planted on earth. His astonishing powers of invention and organization, his command of movement, of grouping, his grasp of textures, his capacity to introduce endless subsidiary elements without interfering with his main theme, and his complete command of his craft never failed him. If sheer ability to create were a test of genius Rubens would be the world's greatest artist (I do not refer to mere fecundity but to the artist's power to find an equivalent in paint for his visual experience). Like his predecessors in Flanders, he is an "eye witness," but an eye witness in the grand manner. If Breughel's secret was affection, Rubens's was enthusiasm—enthusiasm begotten of worldliness, enthusiasm exclusively reserved for earthly things. Flesh he adored and wild movement that gave all his compositions a diagonal sweep. No one can match him in the latter and only Renoir in the former. Where he fails, I think, is not in his inability to leave the earth behind, but in his failure to realize that he could never do so. His Madonnas strike appropriately noble gestures, but they are none the less Flemish wenches who cannot fill those gestures with meaning. Breughel never made that mistake. I have noted elsewhere that in an "Assumption" by Rubens (see Fig. 22) the Madonna flings out her arms in a rhetorical gesture that all grand-mannerists consider suitable to the elevated mood of such a theme, but that she might just as well have done so in order to take a frying-pan off the fire. I find this contradiction the chief impediment to my enjoyment of him. He has every sort of equipment for scaling the heavens— except a pair of wings. And yet he persists in trying to fly. Rubens was in fact the perfect worldling, a good churchman, a devoted husband and father, a successful politician, an excellent business man, an indefatigable worker. Perhaps if he had been a social failure, if he had known a little more suffering, he might have been one of the dozen artists to whom it was permitted to reveal a new world. As it was, he is merely the Prince of Painters.

It is interesting to compare him in this respect with his counterpart in Spain, el Greco. Since the beginning of our own century el Greco's painting has enjoyed an extraordinary popularity, partly for the insufficient reason that twentieth-century art, having discovered the advantages of distortion in the interests of self-expression, and casting round for justification in the art of the past, has found in him the ideal precedent. No great painter, from Giotto to Renoir, has taken more liberties with the human figure, and no great painter has ever created so easily recognizable a set of mannerisms. His colour schemes, his lighting schemes, his system of vertical, rippling composition, the set of flamelike curves he invented are ingredients in the most personal of all styles. If one were to assign a date to him on internal evidence alone one would probably guess that he was a contemporary of Rubens and one would make an error of thirty-two years. In el Greco the Baroque style is as fully developed as it is in Rubens.

There is the same power to contain all the complex elements of the picture within a single embracing phrase, the same sense of a continuous rhythm running through it, the same feeling that the parts have no value except as contributions to the whole. But regarded as personalities no two men could be more different. If Rubens could not soar, el Greco's feet never touch earth. If Rubens's world is earthly, el Greco's is made out of a mixture of ice and flame (see Fig. 21). Rubens's Madonnas and nymphs are Flemish housewives, Greco's have never even heard of a frying-pan. Writers on art, trying to explain this outburst of mysticism, have said much about the ecstatic, mystical flavour of Spanish Christianity, forgetting that when Rubens visited Spain he proved as popular as a painter there as he was in Antwerp, and that no artist could be less mystical than Velasquez. El Greco's ultimate roots in the hieratic Byzantine world are a more probable explanation of his ice-cold ecstasy, his grey-green fire, but surely he needs no explanation. Some artists, like Leonardo and Raphael, are perfect products of their age. Others, like Breughel, are born too late; others, like Giotto, too early. Others again, like el Greco and Blake, are unrelated to their age. It is not necessary to invent a theory to explain them.

El Greco's reputation has always fluctuated with fashionable taste. Not so that of Velasquez (1599–1660), for whom painters and students of every creed have almost always had an unbounded admiration. He is essentially the painter's painter. If, on the evidence of his pictures alone, one would be tempted to put el Greco thirty or forty years later than his actual date, it would be difficult to guess at any date at all for Velasquez. Certainly one would not put him earlier than the last quarter of the Sixteenth Century, but he could equally have belonged to the late Nineteenth Century, not because the late Nineteenth Century copied his way of painting (though Manet did), but because his impersonal, unimpassioned view of life and his complete control of his medium make him dateless. He is as free from mannerisms as el Greco is full of them, dividing his allegiance almost equally between the facts before his eyes and the demands of oil paint. For that reason perhaps art history and art criticism contain few purple passages about his paintings, and yet no critic or historian has failed to admire him. He glorified nothing—neither the earth like Reubens, nor the heavens like el Greco—and falsified nothing. He neither loved nor hated. He did not even comment. He saw things with a steady uncritical eye, and translated them with an unerring hand into paint whose quality is the envy of all painters. He is no mere photographer. He can plan his pictures to a nicety, as an architect might plan a building; but poetry, and the remoter realms of the imagination were beyond him. The famous Rokeby Venus in the National Gallery, compared with a Venus by Titian, is no more than brilliant journalism. In spite of its fame I have always considered it one of his worst paintings with its tired, sagging curves and its efficient, joyless handling of paint, but Velasquez at his best (as in "Las Meninas" or "Las Lanzas" or a portrait like that in Fig. 23), Velasquez aiming imperturbably at a point he is sure of hitting, risking no failures through an attempt at poetry, has no rival.

Spanish painting has always centred itself round the court life of Spain. Dutch painting, even more than Flemish, belonged to the people—the middle-classes of Holland. The hey-day of Dutch painting was short-lived (it covered a period of about fifty years), but those few years saw an extraordinary outburst of artistic activity. For the most part Dutch painting is sober, unspectacular and patient; innumerable little masters recorded its wide skies and low horizons, its homely interiors with their pleasant comfortable inhabitants, their possessions, their hobbies; the same sober domesticity fills all their canvases, giving them a grave, unhurried dignity that occasionallly verges on profundity. It is unnecessary to name these little masters, but among them were one or two of larger stature and one giant.

The earliest of the bigger men was Frans Hals (1580–1666), whose portraits have an unfailing general appeal, though I personally find most of them detestable. They are said to be lively and full of character. Their liveliness seems to me based on a superficial sprightliness and their character on grimace. Hals was certainly a master of brushwork. Facility is his most noticeable characteristic. Peter de Hooch and Terborg, both of whom specialized in painting Dutch householders, would be banal if it were not for their sensitiveness to those elusive shades of gesture and behaviour in everything that is implied by the word domesticity. Without this subtle intimacy (see Fig. 25) they would be lost in the undistinguished mass of anecdotal painting to which their work gave birth. Vermeer of Delft added to their subtlety subtler qualities still—a sense of the fall of subdued light in interiors so finely adjusted that a fly settling on one of his canvases would produce an intolerable disturbance in its balance of hushed, golden tones. To this he added a technique which has always baffled his imitators. It is puzzling to know by what process his translucent, liquid surfaces were achieved. They betray no trace of the human hand at work. His paint seems to have floated miraculously on to the canvas.

The giant of Dutch painting is, of course, Rembrandt. And here the art historian has to gird himself to a special task. Not that there is any difficulty in assessing Rembrandt's stature both as an artist and as a painter. By every known test he is the giant not only of Dutch painting but of European painting. But at this point, in my readers' interests, I must make the confession that I have never been able to love him. Love is an irrational thing, but for the critic it is an essential thing. Without it he may be just but he must inevitably be cold. If a list of the qualities essential to the make-up of every painter were to be drawn up—a list that would include not only purely æsthetic qualities like a sense of colour, of texture, of design, of how most effectively to dispose light and shade, how to suggest volume, recession, movement and so on, but also human qualities like psychological insight or an understanding of the dramatic implication in the scene depicted—and if each painter were to be accorded marks in proportion to his possession of such qualities, Rembrandt would undoubtedly head the list with an accumulation of marks that no other painter could approach. Unfortunately in the presence of such a man the critic begins to suffer from his own limitations. It happens that the particular qualities that appeal most strongly to me are precisely those which Rembrandt lacks—among the æsthetic qualities, that of colour orchestration; among the human qualities, that of gaiety. To feel a little unhappy in the presence of a work of genius which has neither quality is my personal misfortune. Having made this apology I shall cease to obtrude myself and my prejudices and attempt to sum up Rembrandt's achievements by the only method open to me under the circumstances, the method of the examiner who coldly accords marks for excellence.

Rembrandt shared with his Dutch contemporaries their intense love of the sober spectacle of daily life in Holland. Cumulatively the whole school produced a record of the commonplace which only achieved distinction because it approached its task with real devotion and an unusually complete visual equipment. I have already explained (page 41) what I mean by the word "grasp" in its application to the visual world. The Dutch painters possessed this sense of visual values to an unusual degree. With them that sentry in the brain which in most schools of painting refuses to admit certain aspects of visual experience as valid, is almost non-existent. The local visible world in all its aspects is their province, and to none of them more so than to Rembrandt. But whereas in all other Dutch painters this gift was counteracted by a pedestrian quality of imagination, in the case of Rembrandt there was no such disqualification. Within the limits of his sober domestic world he was capable of rising to imaginative heights reached by no other artist. There was no question with him, as there was with the Italians, of creating a race of men and women more aristocratic or more heroic than those of everyday life. Rembrandt took the world as he found it—a queer place full of slums, castles, merchants and beggars—and plunged passionately beneath its surface, extracting from the commonplace a wealth of meaning never suspected before and never exploited since. No one ever worked with a more limited range of subject matter—there is hardly anything in his paintings and drawings that could not be found on his own doorstep or in the houses of his friends or within a mile or so of Leyden or Amsterdam. But no one ever made so much out of so little. His portraits, often of middle-aged or elderly people, homely in both the English and the American sense of the word, have a serene profundity that seem to belong more to the realm of literature than to that of painting (see Fig. 24). In his religious pictures (in which all the *dramatis personæ* are citizens of Amsterdam) Christianity for the first time since Giotto becomes an affair for ordinary men and women. Just as his eye took the whole world of phenomena in its stride, so his mind seems to grasp the whole of human experience of which religion itself is no more than one aspect. Rembrandt's breadth of grasp is, in a sense, puzzling. What is one to make of a man who found as many pictorial possibilities in the interior of an old barn or the flayed carcass of an ox as in the human body or the story of the crucifixion, who can combine in the same canvas a study of the complex and mysterious interplay of light on whatever object happens to lie before him with an essay in psychology or a revelation of human emotion, who can even so contrive it that the one seems merely an aspect of the other, and who is moreover such a superlative craftsman that, without sacrificing freedom and spontaneity of brushwork, he can suggest the warmth, the resilience, the roundness of flesh, the roughness of cloth, the weight of stone, the depth and luminosity of sky?

By the examiner's standards Rembrandt has no rival. And yet how I wish he could give me more pleasure! How I long for him to be not quite such a heavyweight, and, more than anything else, that he could have had the final gift, accorded to so many lesser men—to Matisse, to van Gogh, to Carpaccio, to Fra Angelico for example—of knowing the meaning of the word colour. Rembrandt can do anything except rejoice. There is no nonsense about him: he cannot smile. In that respect alone he is a smaller man than Shakespeare.

It would leave a false impression if nothing were to be said in this chapter about baroque sculpture. There is plenty of it, and of a high order too, but somehow most of it tends to fade from the memory, not because it is not memorable but because it is, in the fundamental sense, baroque. It is almost always a part of a whole, a detail in a larger conception, and it therefore loses its meaning when it is detached from its context. Who can remember the details of the statues on the west front of St. Paul's Cathedral? Yet they are by no means negligible, and the Cathedral would have a bald look without them. Names of baroque sculptors do not leap to the mind, for their work is hardly ever meant to be self-contained. They are like stage designers, working as part of a team, content that their carving should be merged in the bigger ultimate effect.

Yet even as a contributor to an architectural ensemble, Bernini manages to be arresting. In an age that specialized in rhetoric, Bernini's rhetoric is a little more pungent, a little more biting than that of his contemporaries. His statues and groups of statues, his fountains and monuments are *tours de force*, but they are something more. Behind their virtuosity is a kind of swaggering sincerity. Three-dimensional baroque, especially in the churches of Austria and Southern Germany, plunged, at the slightest provocation, into melodrama, but Bernini and the Roman sculptors and sculptor-architects whom he influenced kept their exuberance in check and saved the currency of Italian baroque sculpture from the dangerous consequences of inflation.

CHAPTER XI

PARIS

THE reasons why at a given time a particular country or city should become the radiating point for artistic activity are always complex, but as we have seen, there has been only one period of any considerable length in the history of European art when there was no such single point of radiation. In the interval between the downfall of the Roman Empire and the dawn of the Renaissance political power was too vague to concentrate itself geographically and the organization of the Church was strong enough to distribute itself pretty evenly over the map of Europe. Apart from that period art had always harnessed itself to a cultural centre, and now it was the turn of Paris.

To-day we are so accustomed to thinking of the French as the painterly nation (as Germany is the musical and England the literary nation) that it is a little surprising to find how small a part France has hitherto played in the history of the representational arts. There had been the magnificent outburst that produced the sculptures of Rheims and the windows of Chartres; there had been schools of primitives among which that of Avignon produced one of the world's most moving paintings, the famous "Pietà"; later, the French kings, especially Charles VIII and Francis I, were caught in the spell of the Italian Renaissance. Simone Martini had worked for the Pope in Avignon, and Francis I induced Leonardo to execute commissions for him in France, but there was little enough native French painting or sculpture in the Fifteenth and Sixteenth Centuries, and even in the Seventeenth Italy was still a magnet. In France itself the three brothers Le Nain, ignoring the Italian magnet, painted powerful little pictures of peasant families, pictures whose sinister intimacy and pathos has no apparent connection with the worldliness of the seventeenth century. They reflect what current phraseology would call the underground movement behind the baroque façade. Of the French painters who succumbed to the magnet and spent most of their lives in Italy the most considerable were Nicolas Poussin (1594–1665) and Claude Gelée (1600–1682).

Poussin, like Raphael, had little of his own to contribute to painting. If the history of art is to be considered as a story of conquest, Poussin is nothing, for he made no new discovery. If on the other hand one regards it as a story of achievement he is important in the sense that Raphael is important, as a constructor, an architect of pictures. He would have been supremely happy in the late Fifteenth Century when all things Greek and Roman were tinged with a glamour that goaded artists to a frenzy of production. Poussin was born a hundred years too late. His painstaking, unemotional ingenuity of design has not even the spontaneity of Raphael. What Raphael did by instinct Poussin did by a kind of dogged science. "Je n'ai rien negligé" was his smug comment on himself. One can find no fault with his reconstructions of Arcady except that they are tired. The glamour of Greece has gone, and with it the fervour of the Renaissance. He is rather like an earnest young philanthropist who has inherited a fortune and is determined not to misuse it. The solidity of Florence, the glow of Venice, the enlarged vision of the baroque masters were all at his disposal. He used them with infinite tact and discretion and devitalized them in doing so.

His contemporary, Claude, has some, but not all of the same weaknesses. He at least had the courage to love nature enough to paint landscape for its own sake. It would be untrue to say that he was the first to do so. Rubens had already seen possibilities in landscape, but Rubens had the voracious eye and restless hand that could see possibilities in almost anything. Claude, in concentrating on landscape, took a step that was to have far-reaching consequences, though he himself could not see what those consequences were to be. His own endeavour was not so much to enter into nature's moods as to show that landscape could in itself furnish material for a satisfying picture in the classical manner. He took the hint provided by Giorgione's "Tempest" (see page 87), emptied it of figures, or else reduced the figures to mere accents of colour or tone in the foreground, built up a framework by massing trees or buildings at the sides and then concentrated all his skill on leading the eye inwards through the centre of the picture into vast, light-laden distances. Claude has not the courage to venture right into the heart of untouched nature. For the purposes of painting, seventeenth century nature still has to be dominated by man, with a ruined castle or a Corinthian temple to round off the unruly corners, but one can guess from his drawings that in treating her so he was merely following a convention. Those drawings never fail to evoke the surprised comment, "But how modern!" The notion that a landscape could be a spontaneous expression of a mood or even a topographical record was a much later development and one that Constable was to exploit after nearly two hundred years.

It was not until the end of the Seventeenth Century that France began to produce her own art, and instead of echoing the faded glamour of Italy, reflected the lively if equally artificial life of Versailles. Watteau's short life (1684–1721) makes a bridge between the Seventeenth and the Eighteenth Centuries. He combines the worldliness of the one with the playfulness of the other. But one is interested in Watteau not because he was a representative of his period but because he penetrated beneath its surface. To be sure, the shiny veneer of the early Eighteenth Century at Versailles was not difficult to penetrate; but Watteau penetrated it without hating it or rebelling against it. He accepted court life and court manners without being seduced by them. He is Hamletish in his detachment, but he has none of Hamlet's gloom. He is merely heartbreakingly sad. It is a measure of his greatness that he reminds one of Mozart who can produce just the same effect of hinting at depths beneath the neat, formal pattern of his music. In Watteau's painting the formal pattern of court life is all there—the foppery, the infinite leisure, the endless round of love-for-love's sake, the elegance and the careful avoidance of material discomfort. But behind all that is an acute nostalgia. Nothing lasts. His characters, languid and exquisite, snatch at the fading moment but they cannot arrest it. Death—no, not death; that is too blatant, too real a thing—oblivion rather, is just round the corner lurking behind that shady tree, waiting under the pedestal of the statue of the goddess of Love, ready to steal in and take possession of the scene.

One has to be a little fanciful and Walter Pater-ish in describing Watteau. With other painters a straightforward account of their style and mannerisms will suffice. But with Watteau it is the undertones and overtones that count. Stylistically he was a descendant of Rubens, but one realizes how far removed he was in spirit from Rubens when one finds oneself comparing him to Mozart and Hamlet.

Boucher (1700–1770) has no overtones. He took the Eighteenth Century just as he found it and gave his employer, Madame Pompadour, the exact brand of playful eroticism (thinly disguised as classical mythology) that she wanted. As a boudoir decorator Boucher leaves nothing to be desired. He can be frivolous without being trivial, elegant without being shallow, naughty without being salacious. Fragonard (1732–1800), the last of the true eighteenth-century French painters, has all the sensitiveness and sentiment of Watteau but none of his depth. With him the age of pseudo-Venuses and pseudo-nymphs and shepherds comes to an end. Already even in Fragonard there are hints of a more serious view of life. Love is usually his theme but it is becoming a little less flirtatious, his lovers are not quite so idly engaged in whiling away the time.

I have already pointed out that artistically the Eighteenth Century was not a creative period. Each painter took what he wanted from the material to hand, and out of it evolved a mood that suited the time. There is no such thing as eighteenth-century vision: visual curiosity and æsthetic experiment are alike absent. Their places are taken by the artist's personal reaction to life— Watteau's sadness, Bocher's eroticism, Nattier's flattery, Fragonard's sentiment. Only one painter, Chardin (1699–1779) stands aloof from the rest. Chardin alone interested himself in the more permanent and universal aspects of life, painting a bottle of wine and a loaf of bread with as much interest and affection as he would bestow on a portrait of a mother putting the finishing touches to her little girl's toilette, and finding rich material in both. Chardin's reputation is less than it should be merely because he has so little of the spirit of eighteenth-century Versailles. In outlook he is one of the Dutch masters of a century earlier; his sense of domesticity is as subtle as Terborch's, but, being a Frenchman, his touch is lighter, more elusive, more playful.

French art has always had two characteristics, logic and stylishness. Both are the marks of a civilized people. Logic in French art shows itself in the French artist's habit of formulating a theory before beginning to paint. If Uccello had been a Frenchman he would have foregathered with his friends in the cafés of Montparnasse and announced the birth of a new school of painting—"Perspectivism." Paris has given birth to one "ism" after another in its logical devotion to theory. Stylishness is another matter. It is the result of never allowing the end to be out of tune with the means. Paint is a language: stone is a language. Both speak in visual terms. Paint deals with colour and pattern; stone with shape and mass. Attempt to make those languages express something they were never meant to express and your Frenchman at once loses interest. He has no use for a Blake who tried to make paint behave like literature. Paint, says the Frenchman, is meant to be seen, not read. It deals with qualities like colour, structure, pattern. Hence the stylishness of men like Matisse, Cézanne or Ingres. They attempt to solve no problem that is not a painterly problem.

After the airy Rococo of the Eighteenth Century came the first logical reaction, the Neo-Classic school headed by Jaques Louis David (1743–1825). Neo-Classicism, that curious archaistic movement that resulted from so many divergent causes—the discovery of Herculaneum, the revolt against the frivolity of the court, a dawning sense of Democracy inspired by Rousseau— was very much in the air in the late Eighteenth Century. It was to the political solidity of Rome, not to the cultural splendour of Greece that this subsidiary Renaissance looked. The result was a stiffening up of standards, moral, political and artistic. It is odd that the French Revolution, superficially so wild and dishevelled, should have had an ardent supporter in David whose style was so stiff and precise and so conscientiously noble. One would have expected the Byronic romanticism of Delacroix to have been the kind of painting to accompany a social upheaval. But the romantic wave came later. Ingres (1780–1876), David's pupil, equally conscientious in his classicism, only became human when he had a portrait to paint. Then his sitter, together with his own supple sense of line, melted the hard Neo-Classic crust. Some of his portraits have a flesh-and-blood vitality that is surprising in view of his self-imposed creed.

Delacroix (1798–1863) headed the Romantics, rebelling against his chilly predecessors not only in his subject matter but in his way of painting. Rubens was his ideal as a painter, but he had none of the organizing power of Rubens. Byron was the poet of his choice, but the lonely, wild-eyed Byronic gloom is more effective in literature than in art. Delacroix's method in painting is more interesting than his individual pictures. He is a link in the chain that led finally to Impressionism, but it will be more convenient to consider this aspect of him when dealing with the Impressionists. One massive figure whose whole tendency was romantic but who hides his romanticism under a cloak of satire was Daumier (1808–1879). Most of Daumier's life was occupied in producing many thousands of lithographs for publication in current periodicals. No man who worked as hard as he did could produce masterpieces consistently, but the best of Daumier has the power of strong acid. His subjects were picked from a wide field, but in all of them he concentrated, with an intensity that is often terrifying, on aspects of contemporary life. Scenes from the intimate daily life of working men and women, biting commentaries on the legal profession, scathing political satires poured from his pen day by day and week by week. It was only at the end of his life that he had leisure to paint and freedom to shake off the emotional and propagandist obligations in which the satirist is always involved. In these paintings he reveals himself as a sort of miniature Rembrandt with a passion for the macabre or the picturesque.

Meanwhile, undisturbed by the rival Classic and Romantic factions, a group of painters had withdrawn themselves from Paris and had retired to the country round Barbizon to experiment in a new approach to the painting of landscape. With the Barbizon painters the historian feels that he is at last within measurable distance of his own day. They are the opening paragraphs of his penultimate chapter, and for that very reason they have for us the dowdiness that always belongs to the first beginnings of contemporary things. An early motor-car is dowdier than a stage coach just because the motor-car is part of to-day's currency: the stage coach cannot be old-fashioned, it is merely obsolete. What is "modern" in the Barbizon landscapes is that, unlike those of Claude or even Constable, they were painted on the spot. The contemplative attitude that creeps in as soon as a painter retires to his studio to "build up" a picture from the sketches he has made was never allowed to intervene between them and their paintings. Rousseau, Corot and Millet were the best of them. Rousseau clung with single-minded devotion to nature as he saw it. Corot was a poet who in later life popularized himself by slipping into an easy formula of willow trees and twilight. Millet preached the dignity of peasant labour, and invented that noble stereotyped figure that persists to the present day as a representative of toiling peasanthood and is known to a thousand front parlours through the medium of the "Angelus" and "The Sower." The art of Millet has travelled a long way from the lighthearted naughtiness of Boucher.

Before going on to the history of French Impressionism, the logical successor to the Barbizon School, I must turn back to glance at England.

English painting has a queer, disjointed history. It always seems to be getting into its stride and then exhausting itself. Or else it produces isolated geniuses like Blake or isolated movements like pre-Raphaelitism which refuse to fit into any ready-made art historian's pattern of development. Like France, during the Sixteenth and Seventeenth Centuries, its eyes were turned outwards, but instead of exporting its artists (as France had exported Poussin and Claude) it imported them. Under Henry VIII it was a German, Hans Holbein (1447–1543) who became portrait painter to the king. Rubens visited and worked in England under Charles I, who subsequently appointed a Fleming, Van Dyck, Rubens's pupil, to be his court painter. Under Charles II, Sir Peter Lely, a Dutchman, painted court beauties with conventional stylishness but with quite an exceptional sense of colour. It was not until Hogarth (1697–1764) that England produced an art as native to herself as his contemporary Boucher's was to France. Hogarth was defiantly insular, refused to pay the customary homage to Italy, detested the grand manner, painted vigorous portraits without a hint of flattery and never turned his eyes away from contemporary life. In doing this he became a moralist and was tempted to preach sermons in paint. His pictures are none the worse for that. He is never led away, as Daumier was to be in his lithographs, into flights of moral indignation about the vices of the age. Rather did he see them as amiable, though sometimes sordid weaknesses, and he laughed at them without any undercurrent of indignation. His laughter was hearty and robust. He cannot be dismissed as a "literary" painter, for the adjective only becomes derogatory when paint is misused for ends that could have been better achieved by a novelist or satirist. No artist ever misused paint less than Hogarth. Even the most didactic of his sermons are painterly in conception. His anecdotes are always reconstructions of the drama behind the event, not a superficial rendering of the event itself. His most important innovation was the invention of the "conversation piece," the group in which the personages are linked together by some mildly interesting psychological thread. De Hooch and Vermeer had already pointed the way to this type of painting, but Hogarth gave it a slightly new twist. His conversation pieces have a liveliness and an immediacy that the seventeenth-century Dutchmen never quite achieved.

William Blake (1757–1827) must appear at this point of the narrative, though he has no place in it. Any reference to Blake in a history of art is bound to have the air of a parenthesis, unconnected with what came before or with what was to come after. Blake appears suddenly, *à propos* of nothing, an isolated phenomenon, as disturbing as a meteor to an astronomer engaged in cataloguing the fixed stars.

The masterpieces of European art have usually been biggish things. There is, of course, no particular virtue in size, but if one picks a hundred well-known works at random, ninety of them will probably be more than, say, four feet square. Most of Blake's masterpieces are not much larger than a quarto sheet of paper: some of them (the woodcuts to Thornton's Vergil, for example) have an area of less than three square inches. As compositions they are not particularly original, nor did Blake make any contribution to the vision of his time. Indeed it was impossible for him to do so, for he worked, so to speak, with his eyes shut. The kind of straw of which other artists make their bricks—a well-stocked visual memory—was almost unknown to him. The raw material out of which his drawings were made was of the shoddiest. Never having studied the human figure at first hand, he fell back on engravings after Michelangelo and Raphael and the worn-out architectural idioms of the Gothic revival. With this deplorable equipment, but with an exceptional mastery of line, learned through his training as an engraver, he produced some of the most powerfully evocative drawings ever made. Had he attempted to work on a larger scale the incompleteness of his visual knowledge would probably have betrayed him, but working as he did in water colour or with the engraver's burin he managed to condense whole universes on to a page of a book.

Reynolds (1723–1792) and Gainsborough (1727–1788) are too well known to Englishmen and Americans to need appraisement. What is significant about them as a pair (and their names like those of Dickens and Thackeray are so often linked that one is inclined to think of them as ill-assorted twins) is that they seem to foreshadow the cleavage, frankly admitted to-day, between academic and non-academic art. I shall not attempt to define the terms, but the word academic implies a reverence for the art of the past which too often acts as a brake on spontaneous creative impulse. Academic painters (Reynolds is an excellent example) do frequently succeed in maintaining their own creative head of steam in spite of this reverence: and non-academic painters have been known to fail because they had no sense of tradition to back up their own creative impulses. But it was at about this time that the distinction between the two became apparent. The foundation of Academies of Art in France and England and the new idea that a work of art was a thing to be hung in a public exhibition and not used for a specific private purpose contributed to this distinction between the traditional and the original in art. Reynolds thought (or professed to think) that a portrait could be admirable because it caught the spirit of Raphael or Annibale Carracci: Gainsborough considered that a portrait should catch the spirit of the sitter as seen through the particular temperament of Gainsborough.

I have perhaps overstressed the distinction between the two attitudes in so far as it applies to Reynolds and Gainsborough, but there is a very real and a very disheartening distinction between them to-day. Tradition-worship can be a dangerous thing if the tradition worshipper forgets that new tradition can only be brought into being by men whose reverence for old traditions can give way before their urgent desire to create something of their own. No one would deny that if Giotto had felt more respect for Byzantine tradition, or if Bellini had not outgrown his reverence for Mantegna, European painting would be considerably poorer. And yet our contemporary academies are filled with work that adds nothing (because it has nothing to add) to the Impressionist tradition established by Monet and Pissarro sixty years ago.

Impressionism as a name dates back to 1874; but as a way of looking at nature its roots can be traced as far back as the beginnings of baroque art. Many of Michelangelo's unfinished statues are impressionistic in essence; so is most of Titian's late work. All Constable's innovations led in the direction of impressionism. Delacroix's modifications of Rubens's technique came from hints picked up by Delacroix from Constable. Turner's work from, say, 1840 onwards is purely impressionist in method though not in intention.

Impressionism, as a self-conscious creed, is simply an attempt to emphasize a particular aspect of visual truth that had been either overlooked or not consciously emphasized by previous painters. By the year 1863 the sentry (see p. 73) which only allows the visual messages transmitted by the eye to penetrate to the brain after a rigorous censorship, had admitted most aspects of visual truth by a process of gradual infiltration, but there were two that had not yet officially passed the censor. They were (1) the colour and vibration of light and (2) the density of air. No one had ever painted the true colour of sunshine and shadow, no one had fully exploited the sensation that light *dances* (though Watteau, Constable and Delacroix had all hinted at it) and hardly anyone had thought it worth while to suggest that the density of the air is not always constant, that a picture could be painted, for instance, of a landscape seen through a heavy mist or fog. These problems were tackled by Claude Monet (1840–1926) and Camille Pissarro (1831–1903) to the exclusion of a great many of the qualities which previous artists had considered essential. What made their pictures seem queer and unacceptable to their contemporaries was as much the omission of these old qualities as the inclusion of the new ones. If, for example, Monet had built up his compositions on Classical lines with a stone pine on one side and a ruined temple on the other, instead of painting a haystack at sunrise or a slice of the west front of Rouen Cathedral at sunset, the storm aroused by the first impressionist pictures might have been avoided. But it was by no means the first storm of the kind. When Constable tried to render the exact state of the English weather, the tumbled clouds, the vivid green meadows, the foliage of trees sparkling as it moved in the wind, and when he evolved for this purpose a nervous, shimmering brush-stroke, with broken tones flicked with pure white, there was plenty of violent protest, although Constable was experimenting solely in the interest of truth. Turner was not so universally misunderstood. Ruskin's enthusiastic championship of him is apt to give the impression that he had no other champion than Ruskin, but Turner was in fact a highly successful artist. His success, I imagine, was due to the fact that the English public has always succumbed to the poetical, good or bad, in painting; it liked Turner because he stressed the romantic and the picturesque in landscape. Ruskin saw that behind Turner's romance and picturesqueness was an extraordinary grasp of the structure of a landscape, but even Ruskin withdrew his approval when in his later life Turner's landscapes began to melt away—to be eaten up, as it were, by the radiance of light and the envelope of air. Constable recorded with all the skill at his command the particular type of weather on the particular day. Turner generalized his weather, but concentrated on new and impressive ways of painting light.

The French Impressionists naturally admired Constable more than Turner, for their whole intention was to be accurate, not impressive. Yet in the end they came nearer to Turner than to Constable. Monet, at the end of *his* life, was producing work that had a strange resemblance to Turner's, though he arrived at it by a different set of means. The West front of Rouen Cathedral, seen throuth the red haze of sunset by the analytical eye of Monet (see Fig. 27), was very like the same scene viewed by the romantic eye of Turner. Truth, under certain conditions, can be as strange as poetry and as impressive.

There is no need to repeat here what was said in an earlier chapter (see page 44) about the effect of Impressionism on the painter's palette. But it is worth repeating that Impressionism furnishes the clearest instance in the history of art of a new visual discovery, made in a spirit of pure research, which produced in the long run a new kind of beauty. In the short run it produced what most critics of the 1860's were pleased to regard as a new type of ugliness. To them it seemed ugly, not because its colour schemes were more violent and its outlines more vague than in the art with which they were familiar, but simply because they themselves were too insensitive to recognize the essential truth of these new qualities, and because they were still hankering after their tree in the foreground and open space in the centre.

Impressionism then is the final attempt of the Nineteenth Century to paint just what the eye sees. "Monet is only an eye. But what an eye!" said Cézanne, fastening in these few words on the virtues and weaknesses of the whole school. The virtues were that it enlarged visual experience, widened the bracket once more. Its chief weakness was that its exponents were entirely at the mercy of nature. The *kind* of truth it fastened on was the truth of the passing moment, the "impression" that a man would retain on his retina if he allowed himself to look at a given scene for a few seconds only. The brooding, contemplative attitude (which accounts, for instance, for Turner's later paintings of light) is utterly rejected by the Impressionists. Monet carried out the Impressionist programme conscientiously. Realizing that daylight changes its character with each passing cloud, each shift of the sun in the heavens, he began his day's work with a series of canvases, each one to be worked on for no more than a quarter of an hour. It was the painter's supreme attempt at complete objectivity. If nature, during any particular quarter of an hour, was "off colour" (and nature is often guilty of surprising lapses) Monet would blindly follow her into a morass of chromatic bad taste. His own sense of colour harmony was deplorable. Camille Pissarro had not quite the same brilliantly objective attitude to paintings; in him there is an undercurrent of affection that tempers the ruthless analysis of Monet. Sisley (1839–1889) was an equally clear observer, but his range was narrower; he was content to record the more "normal" conditions of light and in consequence his landscapes avoid the appearance of being "stunts" that Monet's often give.

These three formed the shock troops of Impressionism. Manet (1832–1883) and Degas were associated with the movement but they specialized less furiously in telling the Impressionist truth and nothing more. They were better artists if only because their interests ranged beyond the mere "look" of things. Complete objectivity is in the nature of things an impossibility; even the camera cannot achieve it, for the man behind the camera who selects his length of exposure, his subject matter, his time of day, cannot help imposing his choice even on the machine. As far as a human being can achieve it, Manet did so. Before him perhaps Velasquez was the painter who least obtrudes his own temperament, and it was to Velasquez that Manet turned at first, and it was as a homage to Velasquez rather than to Titan that he painted his "Olympia" (Fig. 20). He was more conscious of the impact of light than Velasquez, and of the way in which light interferes with local colour, but he did not adopt the 'divisionist' technique by which Monet strove to render the vibration of light. Degas arrived by a different route at the effect given by the Impressionists, of having taken a random eyeful of nature and pinned it with one swift movement on to canvas. Degas was not particularly interested in the impact of light, but he was fascinated by something equally transient—the unpremeditated gesture of everyday life, women trying on hats, girls ironing at a laundry, dressing, undressing, dancers in the queer momentary poses of the ballet, horses on the racecourse. His eye pounced with the swiftness of a hawk on such fragmentary gestures, and he gave them an additional air of naturalness by picking up at least one hint from the camera. The camera cannot compose a picture. It merely takes a portion of what is before it and cuts it off like a slice of cake. It has no compunction in slicing, say, right through a figure; it has no sense of balance, of symmetry. Out of this haphazard treatment Degas evolved a new system of composition. He gives the impression of a snapshot, casual and fortuitous, but for all that there is nothing casual in his design. The balance is as careful as in any composition by Titian, and much more daring. I have no space to analyse his pictures here, nor is it necessary to do so. What I wish to point out is that Degas made a subtle art of seeming casual. His characters have the air of being taken unawares, yet they never have that appearance which the camera invariably gives, of having been frozen in mid-gesture. Degas's most able follower was the English Sickert, who, without having Degas's hawk-like pounce, sees life in much the same way—taking unawares the fascinating little accidents that make up its sum; Degas recorded them with some measure of disillusionment. Sickert did it with a kind of painterly chuckle.

The reader may perhaps have gathered from my introductory chapters that this intense pursuit of the thing seen that characterizes the whole of the Impressionist movement is not particularly sympathetic to me. For me, brilliant as the best exponents of Impressionism were, there is something essential that they lack. Call it faith if you like, though faith is rather too narrow a word. Merely to record, to be "only an eye" is not quite enough. If you ask me what else they could have done, what kind of faith they could have served by their art, in what way they could have harnessed themselves to the less superficial strata of life, I cannot answer. I can only say that the men who came after them, the Post-Impressionists, seem to me to penetrate deeper. Perhaps

I can make the distinction clearer by saying that when Cézanne or van Gogh painted they *created* something, whereas Monet and Sisley merely *caught* something. That, of course, is only half the truth, but it is an important half-truth to grasp. It consti- tutes the turning point, as I see it, in the whole direction of art at the end of the Nineteenth Century. It is perhaps too early to be dogmatic, but I believe that with Cézanne the pendulum that Giotto started swinging in the direction of realism came to a pause and that it has now begun to swing back, just as it did at the beginning of the Byzantine era.

Monet and Degas snatched at visual experience; Cézanne and Picasso construct and reconstruct *on a basis* of visual experience. In doing so they are far closer to the main tradition of art than their predecessors.

The one Parisian artist in the Impressionist group who is firmly established in the main tradition is Renoir, who cared nothing for Impressionist theories but made free use of the Impressionist palette and its heightened range of colour. One cannot imagine Renoir bothering his head about any artistic theory. Paint to him was a medium—the only possible medium—for expressing his worship of femininity. In his particular sense of the splendour of the human body he was almost a Greek, but instead of think- ing of it as a noble splendour he felt it as an adorable splendour. His women are not goddesses like Titian's, nor bourgeois amazons like Rubens's, they are not naughty like Boucher's, nor dainty like Watteau's. They are women seen as a child might see its mother, soft and rounded and radiant (see Fig. 28). All Renoir's paintings have this quality of radiance—his landscapes and his portraits as well as his *baigneuses*. Above all, Renoir's art was the exact opposite of Monet's, in that it was not at all concerned with the transient. His sunshine is eternal sunshine, and even though, for him, femininity happened to have taken up its abode in the ample pink and white body of his cook, it was still the eternal feminine.

I have written as though the only significant art produced by the Nineteenth Century were Impressionist. That is not quite true. From my chapter on Spain I have omitted Goya, the last twenty-six years of whose life were lived in the Nineteenth Century. And from my digression on English Nineteenth Century paintings I have omitted the Pre-Raphaelites, Whistler, and G. F. Watts, who seems to me to be suffering at present from an undeserved eclipse.

Goya (1746–1826), the last great Spaniard, forms a link between the Eighteenth and Nineteenth Centuries, much as Watteau does between the Seventeenth and Eighteenth or el Greco between the Sixteenth and Seventeenth. And like both of them he is a lonely figure, too personal to fit into the spirit of his day, and yet compelled to serve a Royal patron. How he managed to retain his position as court painter when he so consistently refused to flatter his sitters is a mystery. His big group of King Charles IV and the whole Spanish royal family is an exasperated commentary on small vices—meanness, bad temper, snobbishness, arrogance, self-indulgence. When his bitterness is not aroused Goya is a superb and sympathetic portrait painter, second only to Rembrandt in profundity, ahead of Hogarth in liveliness. His portraits are all of people thinking, talking, explaining—being themselves in fact, not merely sitting for their portraits. And the pearly, unforced quality of his paint makes Gainsborough look coarse by comparison. Goya was a robust hater of hateful things. He had none of Hogarth's laughter. In his etchings, "The Disasters of the War," he omits nothing in the emotional sequence that runs from pathos to tragedy, from indifference to ultimate cruelty.

Out of the general dull level plain of English nineteenth century painting rise three minor but interesting protuberances. On the subject of the pre-Raphaelite Brotherhood I find it difficult to write without bias. So many contemporary critics whose opinions I usually respect are apt to dismiss the whole movement with an exclamation of impatient scorn that I am alternately tempted to overpraise it and to wonder whether I am a victim of one of those unreasoning loyalties that have their roots in a childhood's love. Granted that British art tends to have a literary flavour, and that the pre-Raphaelites can be as anecdotal as Hogarth and more literary than any other set of painters in history, I cannot see why they should for that reason be scorned as artists. All painters (with the exception of certain twentieth-century puritans who will be mentioned in the next chapter) have been, *au fond*, illustrators. Giotto describing the meeting of the Virgin Mary and St. Anne, or Chardin describing the texture of a loaf of bread are both equally engaged in a descriptive task. They are not better or worse painters for having done so. What made them good painters was their power to find equivalents in paint for their feelings about the Visitation or a cottage loaf. Both of them felt intensely, both of them visualized completely and both of them were good crafts-men. To my mind the pre-Raphaelites at their best pass all three tests with honour, and at their worst they are a little better than their contemporaries.

The movement was not a simple one. It started as a protest against the artificiality of the "grand manner," which, in the eyes of Millais and Holman Hunt, had its origins in Raphael. It was a plea for honest, searching vision that avoided nothing, omitted nothing and above all conventionalized nothing. Hence their passion for detail and their devotion to the particular as opposed to the general or the ideal. Their impatience with post-Raphaelite art led them to study the Italian and Flemish primi-tives, but having none of the instinctive Italian largeness and nobility, it was from van Eyck and his kind that they had most to learn. They were, in fact, "eye witnesses" in exactly the same spirit as the Flemish primitives. But in addition to this (purely æsthetic) motive force they had a streak of romanticism of an escapist kind which attracted them into a past of their own imagining. They projected themselves into a mediæval world of vivid colour and stressed pattern and even at first adopted a certain archaistic Gothic gaucherie, though their own acuteness of observation never allowed this to go too far. Millais entered this mediæval world through the poems of Keats, Rossetti through those of Dante, Burne Jones through his admiration of Rossetti. Holman Hunt, the pedestrian of the party, never shared this romanticism; Madox Brown, the psychologist of the group (see Fig. 26), used the pre-Raphaelite formula with a strongly personal twist.

But in spite of their escapism and their mannerisms I am convinced that the best of their work is immortal, for they were escaping *to* something that they adored and their mannerisms were founded on an emotional intensity that is rare in art. Madox Brown's "Work" and his frescoes in the Manchester Town Hall, Millais's "Autumn Leaves" and his "Lorenzo and Isabella," and Rossetti's early watercolours are original works of art of very high order. I suspect that the present fashionable attitude to the pre-Raphaelites is partly due to the accident that none of their best paintings happen to be in London and partly to the fact that in the later stages of the brotherhood all its members fell from grace. Millais lost his ardour, Holman Hunt descended into sentimentality, Rossetti became the slave of his own mannerisms, Burne Jones's world of dreams degenerated into a world of fancy dress.

G. F. Watts (1817–1904) is equally under a cloud to-day but for a different reason. He was not an illustrator but a preacher, an allegorist, with a moral to be read in each of his allegories. Chesterton, in an essay on Watts which entirely overlooks his merits as a painter, has pointed out in some detail how thoughtful his allegorical essays were. Chesterton is right, but Watts could have been an atrociously bad artist for all that. Unlike the pre-Raphaelites he had no prejudice against the grand manner. In fact it is precisely because he was one of those rare spirits to whom the grand manner came quite naturally (certainly the only one in the history of British painting) that he is so considerable a figure. To compare him with Titian would be absurd, though he has some of Titian's grandeur and breadth. What makes him memorable is his command of impressive gesture, not the empty rhetorical gesture of Michelangelo's followers, but the unexpected attitude that conveys a state of mind or of character. Good examples of this power are the outstretched threatening arm of Death in his "Love and Death" and the bowed back of the rich man in "For he had Great Possessions."

Whistler is not yet outmoded. The Twentieth Century likes Whistler. He was impish, a cynic, a poseur, a rebel, but, like Velasquez and Manet, a remarkably able painter. Had he been a contemporary of Velasquez he would probably never have been heard of, for he would have had nothing to rebel against, no target for his cynicism, no one to shock with his acid witticisms. But he came just at the right time to prick the bubble of Victorian priggishness and to preach the doctrine of "art for art's sake." Japanese prints and willow-pattern china made an innocent enough background for his æstheticism, which he somehow contrived to make positively naughty. He managed to turn himself into a legend that still lives by the simple expedients of being a dandy, possessing a caustic wit and calling his pictures "symphonies." His chief contribution to nineteenth-century English painting is to have brought back simplicity to it, at a time when it was frittering itself away on making painstaking records of trivial detail. The battle that Whistler fought, and won, in England had already been won by Manet in France. Someone had to prick the Victorian bubble in England, and no one was more competent to do so than Whistler, but the bubble would eventually have deflated itself in any case. Whistler was an ambassador rather than a leader.

CHAPTER XII

THE ART OF THE TWENTIETH CENTURY

I wish the word "modern" could have been spared the connotations it is burdened with to-day. Those connotations are, however, inevitable. There have been certain moments in the history of art when the word was bound to take on a more definite, more violent meaning—the moment, for instance, when Myron produced his "Discobolus," when the Mausoleum of Galla Placidia was completed, when the Arena Chapel at Padua was first opened. To-day the word conveys the same specialized sense of old traditions broken and new paths opened up, but to-day one can point to no particular moment that marked the change. Lexicographers will be able to trace the gradual shift at the turn of the century in the use of the word "modern." In architecture the break with the past took the form of a self-conscious revolt based on slogans like "fitness for purpose" or aphorisms like Corbusier's "A house is a machine for living in," but in painting and sculpture the new outlook appeared without a slogan. Both Cézanne and van Gogh began by using an existing technique, the Impressionist technique, and the general public hardly noticed that after six hundred years of steady movement the pendulum had begun to swing back once more. Van Gogh continued till his death to use Impressionist mannerisms for non-Impressionist ends; Cézanne eventually abandoned them as unsuitable to his purpose. A few artists and a few critics saw what was happening, but the first beginnings of "modernism" in the representational arts were not spectacular enough to create any general stir. Whereas the Impressionists had been reviled, Cézanne, during his lifetime, was hardly noticed. What eventually gave "modernism" the appearance of a complete *volte-face* was not the earnest experiment of Cézanne, but the work of certain painters who saw the direction in which Cézanne was moving, and pursued that direction with a logical thoroughness that changed the whole character of painting and sculpture. Cézanne himself would certainly have been puzzled had he lived to see the fruits of his life's work. He thought of himself as a stern traditionalist; his aim was to be another Poussin, but a Poussin whose eyes were fixed on nature instead of on Raphael. No creed could be less revolutionary than his and yet within a few

years of Cézanne's death Picasso was painting pictures based on
Cézanne that seemed to have no connection with pictures painted
in any previous period (see Figs. 29, 30).

This chapter must be brief. The century is only forty years
old, and though each of those forty years has seen a vast out-
pouring of painting and sculpture, not very much of it will be
regarded by critics of the future as being truly twentieth-century
in flavour. To submit this output to a detailed sifting would
be to lose one's sense of proportion in so brief a sketch of the
art of civilized Europe. So far only three names have been
mentioned in this chapter. I shall mention no more, but try
to assess the kind of change that has taken place and to discuss
the reasons for it.

If I were asked for a word to describe the general temper of
twentieth-century art, I should (after some hesitation) choose
"puritanism." Puritanism is that attitude of mind which singles
out an essential quality and refuses to enrich it with subsidiary
qualities. The puritan declares, for example, that the essential
quality in religion is an ethical standard with which nothing
must be allowed to interfere. He refuses to allow art, mysticism
or ritual to reinforce the central ethical idea. He refuses to allow
his idea of goodness to be anthropomorphized by art, or to
permit the emotional appeal of art to interfere with his ethical
conception of religion. The puritan detests complexity. He wants
life to be on a single level, without overtones, without irrelevances.
He makes his decision as to what is desirable, isolates it and
clings to it with a rigid simplicity that finds no room for the kind
of human weakness that is always tempted into bypaths. The
Greek with his physical standard, the Cromwellian with his moral
standard, were equally puritan in that they allowed nothing to
turn their creed into a compromise. The Gothic spirit, on the
other hand, and that of the High Renaissance are rich in compromise. Both recognized the complexity of life with its contradictory claims of body and soul, instinct and reason, laughter
and tears. The modern artist (partly from choice and partly
from necessity) has adopted an æsthetic standard which gives
his work an unusual narrowness and at the same time an unusual
intensity both of which are essentially puritan.

Throughout this book I have tried to stress the complex nature
of the representational arts. The artist continually finds himself
forced to reconcile the conflicting claims of symbolism and
realism (the discovering of a visual equivalent for an emotional
state on the one hand and the representation of a visible fact

on the other), to compromise between the expression of his own experience and the demands of the cause he serves, between art as a reference-to-life and art as a thing-in-itself. Each of these three conflicting interests sets up a kind of internal tug-of-war in the artist, and the modern artist has made up his mind in all three cases as to which side he is prepared to back.

(1) Symbolism *versus* Realism. If realism (i.e. the representation of recognizable objects seen more or less impartially, as the camera would see them, or as the Impressionists tried to see them) is to have a place in his work, it must be a secondary place. If he has an emotional bias, the representation of fact must be subordinated to the demands of his emotional state. In this he is an Expressionist rather than an Impressionist, a disciple of el Greco rather than of Velasquez.

(2) Self-expression *versus* Social Demands. This, of course, is closely related to No. 1, but it is a problem that solves itself in the world of to-day almost without the need of decision on the part of the artist. Society has, in most directions, ceased to make any demands on the artist, leaving him largely free to express himself without reference to his social background. The change is by no means a modern one. Post-Pagan but Pre-Renaissance art, harnessed as it was almost exclusively to the Christian church, was under the strictest obligation to provide religious propaganda either by establishing an emotional mood (as the Byzantine mosaics did) or by its powers of narrative, especially valuable to a society that was mainly illiterate. Under such conditions the subject-matter of art was inevitably as important as its power to communicate the artist's particular brand of visual experience. To-day those conditions have almost ceased to exist. To-day a prospective purchaser will ask for "a Cézanne" because what he wants is a sample of the Cézannesque. But one cannot imagine a fourteenth-century client asking for "a Simone Martini" when what he really wanted was "a Madonna and Child with St. Francis." The shift in emphasis from subject-matter to style has been gradual but steady and the reasons for the shift are not difficult to discover. The church's grip over the artist was considerably loosened by the Renaissance. It was replaced by civic power in sixteenth-century Venice, by the middle classes in seventeenth-century Holland, by the Court in eighteenth-century France, by the aristocracy and plutocracy in eighteenth-century England and finally by nothing at all in the nineteenth century, unless one regards commerce as the true patron of nineteenth-century art and modern posters as the

legitimate successors to the Christian narrative pictures of Giotto, the patriotic rhetoric of Venice, the genre pictures of Holland, the elegant fantasies of Watteau or the portraits of Gainsborough.

No one, however, would cite the modern poster as typical of the best of twentieth-century art in the sense that the narrative pictures of Giotto were typical of the best of fourteenth-century Italian art. The art of to-day at its best is not produced to supply a demand. It is the expression of the inner vision of a man who has no longer any need to bother about society. If the artist is interested in the spectacle of life it is his own private interests that he depicts on canvas. Degas painted his ballet girls and *femmes au tub* not because his patrons asked him to do so, but because movement and gesture fascinated him. But Cézanne's detachment was even more complete. He studied his landscapes or his fragment of still-life or his sitter in a spirit of pure research, reducing all three to their simplest terms (see Fig. 29), dehumanizing them in just the same way as a medical student must dehumanize the body he is dissecting. Cézanne's portraits of his wife shed no light on the character of Madame Cézanne: they even tell one very little about her outward appearance. His still-lifes of apples and jugs have none of the lovable atmosphere that clings about those of Chardin. They are starting-points for a problem in æsthetics, essays in roundness or hollowness or density. It is possible that had Paolo Uccello or Piero della Francesca had the same freedom from social obligations as Cézanne, they, too, would have pursued the same puritanical course, caring for nothing but abstractions like perspective or structure or the relationships of objects in space. But they could not have the same freedom. They had also to consider the claims of the Church, the purity of the Madonna or the mystery of the Resurrection. They were forced, in a word, to be human beings as well as artists. No artist who thought of his art as being concerned with form alone would have been tolerated by the art patron of the Italian Renaissance.

(3) Art-as-reference-to-life *versus* art-as-a-thing-in-itself. This, again, follows from what I have said above. The moment art ceased to be under the direct control of a social force like the church, the state, the king or the merchant, the artist ceased to be responsible to anyone but himself. Art tended therefore to become an affair of the laboratory, just as the scientist's research into the nature of electricity would become a matter of pure theory if the demand for electric light or heat or power were to

cease. Under such conditions theory is bound to flourish and the practical application of theory to suffer a setback. It is no wonder, therefore, that Cézanne's followers produced a plentiful crop of -isms, new ways of visual thinking, new ways of translating their visual thinking into paint. Cézanne's preoccupation with structure could hardly fail to become exaggerated into Cubism. His delight in reducing the object painted to its simplest terms was bound to result in abstract art—art which discarded the object itself even as a starting point, and pursued purely formal ends just as music pursues formal ends. Such freedom to experiment is an excellent thing provided it is eventually used as a means and not as an end in itself. The last thirty years have seen an immense stride forward in the painter's control over form and colour. New types of composition have been explored, new chromatic possibilities opened up, a new visual world based on the engineering side of painting has come into being. Where Raphael and el Greco could only throw out hints by the way, Picasso can devote his whole inventive energy to such problems, and the results have been truly revolutionary and immensely exciting (see Fig. 30). At present we can only dimly grasp the new possibilities. Future generations of painters will doubtless exploit these pioneer discoveries and apply them once more to what is clumsily called "life." At present we stand on the threshold and peer dimly into the future. I feel convinced that the art of the next century will be very different in kind from that of the last six centuries, just as Byzantine art was different from Hellenic art. At present it is at the cross roads. It still retains and uses much nineteenth-century currency; Impressionism is still a living, though I think it is a dying language.

The last few years have seen a new experiment, a new form of puritanism, namely Surrealism. My own attitude to the surrealist creed is that it may be profoundly interesting as a branch of psychology, but that it can only be art by accident— the accident that the Surrealist may perhaps also be an artist. Surrealism insists that the all-important factor in painting is subject-matter, and that the subject-matter should be based on the symbolism provided by the unconscious mind's eye. In its insistence on the importance of subject-matter Surrealism differs in no respect from the most regrettable phases of mid-Victorian painting. In its obsession with Freudian psychology it merely takes one element that has been a constant ingredient in the art of the past and enlarges it to the exclusion of all other elements. Hieronymus Bosch, Breughel and many of the Gothic artists drew freely on the dream-world for their subject-matter. Their only difference from the Surrealists is that they did not disclaim any æsthetic intention nor did they refuse to link up the unconscious life with the conscious.

None the less even Surrealism has had its influence on the art of to-day in creating a new sensitiveness to the possibilities of subject-matter just as abstract art has created a new sensitiveness to the possibilities of form.

As to the future of painting and sculpture in Europe I can venture no prophecy. Given three fixed points, a curve can be drawn to run through them and continue beyond them, but given only two, any number of curves is possible, and, as I see it, twentieth-century art has only just reached the second point. It has progressed away from late nineteenth-century romanticism. Its direction has been steadily towards puritanism of outlook and classicism of form. It concerns itself with essentials, not with accidents; with generalizations, not with particular instances; with fundamentals, not with surface truths; with things digested by the mind, not merely seen by the eye. It has, in fact, retraced its steps from the purely visual world of nineteenth-century art and is far more in tune with the formalized world of Byzantine and Mediæval art. Picasso's experiments in formalization would, I am sure, be more comprehensible to the mosaicists of Santa Prassede than they are to the generation that was brought up on Impressionism.

But what distinguishes the art of to-day from mediæval art is its motive-force. I cannot believe that any branch of art can base itself for long mainly on æsthetic research. To do so is to live in an ivory tower. Art must link itself firmly to something outside itself, and at present it is impossible to see what that something will be. To-day, I believe, for the first time in history, a style has been born that is not the result of pressure from outside. It is a style that has been evolved by the artist left to himself. It is a language constructed not by men of faith for the expression of a particular set of ideas, but by grammarians for the sake of its own flexibility. Inevitably the layman complains that the artist as grammarian does not interest him: that what does interest him is the artist's power to use his language for the interpretation of human experience: and that, on the whole, modern art fails to exploit that power.

Ten years ago the complaint was justified. To-day (I am adding this final paragraph in January 1945) in a country that has spent five years in cultural isolation from the continent of Europe, the cause for the complaint is breaking down. What has been happening to art on the continent I do not know, but in England two factors have altered the relationship between the artist and his social background. One is the new attitude of the State towards the artist. The State has begun to take its responsibilities as patron of the arts more seriously. The War Artists' Committee has provided some of our best painters with a theme and with a job. C.E.M.A. (the Council for the Encouragement of Music and the Arts) has provided machinery whereby exhibitions of painting and sculpture circulate throughout England in towns and villages which had previously no opportunity of seeing contemporary work. Even more important is the emotional impact of the war on artist and layman alike. More and more the artist of to-day tends to take as his subject a set of experiences familiar to everyone. The tension, the tragedy, the urgency of modern war cannot be dealt with in terms of pure aesthetics. The needed pressure from outside has come, and it has humanized the artist and drawn him a good deal closer to the layman.

Admittedly it is a temporary pressure. It would be lamentable if the potency of art were to depend on the continuance of human suffering. But it is possible that out of the present suffering will emerge an intensification of faith, and that the renewed faith will take art into its service as faiths have invariably done in the past.

What form the new faith will take is more than I can guess; still less can I predict what form will be taken by the art that will serve it.

CHAPTER XIII

NOTE ON THE DIAGRAM

SOME apology is due for the unshapeliness of the Diagram below, but I would rather it were unshapely than uninformative. The information it is intended to convey is complex, though I have reduced its complexity to a minimum. If I had attempted to work it out in greater detail it would have become impossibly intricate.

The diagram is concerned with the chief schools of European painting from Giotto to the present day. It attempts to indicate:

(a) Their relative importance (by the area of the shaded masses).

(b) Their approximate dates (see the figures in the left-hand column).

(c) The principal artists (each represented by a circle).

(d) Their relative importance (by the size of the circle).

(e) Their dates (the centre of each circle is placed on the central point of the artist's productive life), and

(f) The threads of influence between schools and between artists.

I had intended to work out the diagram on the basis of my simile of a river, but the development of artistic traditions is not quite as simple as the course of a river. A river springs from its own tributaries, but it cannot split into tributaries. Artists not only assimilate the influence of previous artists: they also radiate their own influence. Moreover, a map of a river system gives no indication of the force of the current.

As the diagram is largely based on my personal opinions, each reader will doubtless wish to modify it to suit his own. Is Goya really so detached from the main current? Is Hogarth as big as the diagram suggests? And is Cézanne as small? Had Holbein no artistic progeny? Are the pre-Raphaelites worth including?

One aspect of the diagram is bound to be particularly controversial. I have been rash enough here (by the size of the circles) to indicate my own estimate of their "importance." If I am asked what principle has guided me in making this estimate, I can only reply that "importance" in any given case depends on so many factors that there can be no question of following a principle. Michelangelo, for example, is a limited artist, but so powerful within his limitations that he must be given the highest rank. Whistler would probably not have been included at all had he been born at any other time: his importance depends on his contrast with his contemporaries. Caravaggio's claim to inclusion is based entirely on his influence on Velasquez. Poussin depends on his ingenuity and integrity (and not at all on his originality); Cézanne on the impetus he gave to his followers. Rubens's fame rests on the cumulative effect of a mass of work, Masaccio's on the intensity of a tiny handful of frescoes, Vermeer's on his perfection, Constable's on his honesty, Turner's on his imaginative vision. Holbein is great because he faced up so squarely to the world he lived in, el Greco because he created a new one.

I am aware that the diagram gives the impression that all the giants of European art belong to the fairly remote past and that the Nineteenth and Twentieth Centuries have been only productive of talent or mediocrity. That is inevitable, since the stature of genius depends as much on the existence of opportunity as on the power to seize it. In the Sixteenth Century Renoir would probably have been as big a man as Titian because Venice would have used him to better purpose than Paris did. In an age in which the artist is no longer a major ingredient in the social fabric it is difficult for him to attain to full stature. He is driven either to æsthetic experiment on the one hand or to the purely personal expression of his own temperament on the other, and in neither case can he develop his full potentialities. Isolated instances do still occur of artists who have been provided with big opportunities, even in the Twentieth Century—Picasso's "Guernica," Spencer's Burghclere Chapel, Rivera's Mexican frescoes and, within the last two years, the official British war artists are examples—but they are the exception, not the rule.

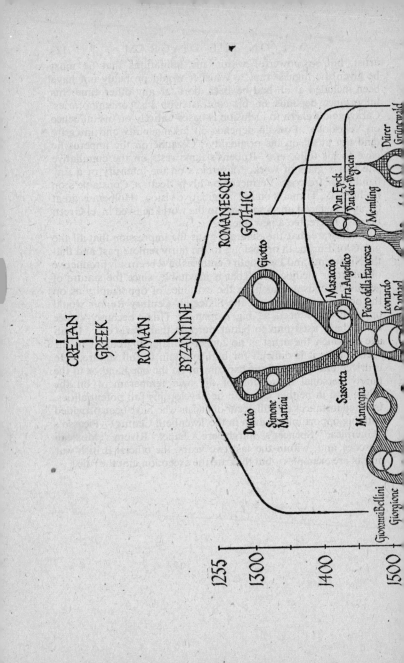

CRETAN
GREEK
ROMAN
BYZANTINE

ROMANESQUE
GOTHIC

Duccio
Simone
Martini

Mantegna

Sassetta

Giotto

Masaccio
Fra Angelico

Piero della Francesca

Leonardo
Pollaiuolo

Van Eyck
Van der Weyden

Memling

Dürer
Grünewald

Giovanni Bellini
Giorgione

1255
1300
1400
1500

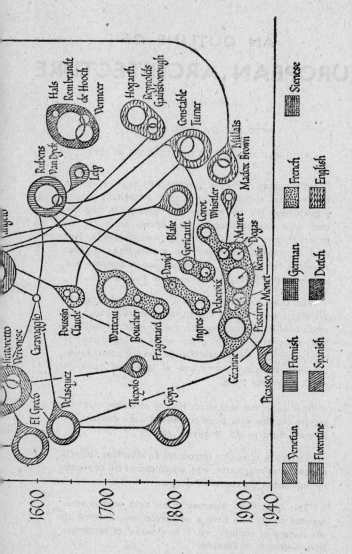

1600

1700

1800

1900
1940

Tintoretto
Veronese

Caravaggio

El Greco
Velásquez

Tiepolo

Goya

Poussin
Claude

Watteau
Boucher
Fragonard

David
Ingres
Delacroix

Blake
Géricault

Corot
Whistler

Manet
Renoir Degas
Pissaro Monet

Cézanne

Picasso

Rubens
Van Dyck
Lely

Hals
Rembrandt
de Hooch
Vermeer

Hogarth
Reynolds
Gainsborough

Constable
Turner

Millais
Madox Brown

Venetian

Florentine

Flemish

Spanish

German

Dutch

French

English

Sienese

A Pelican Book (A 109)

AN OUTLINE OF
EUROPEAN ARCHITECTURE

by Nikolaus Pevsner

REVISED AND ENLARGED EDITION

WITH 48 PLATES AND 60 ILLUSTRATIONS IN TEXT

This is a history of Western architecture as an expression of Western civilisation, described historically in its growth from the 9th to the 19th century. It does not deal with the architecture of classical antiquity, or, generally, with that of the first thousand years A.D. Nor does it attempt to cover the architecture of those countries which have developed under oriental and Byzantine influences, Russia and the Balkan lands.

With these exceptions, it tells the story of European architecture during the last thousand years through the medium of its outstanding expressions in actual building. Not every architect or every work of importance is mentioned: but the styles discussed and the points raised are illustrated by descriptions of individual buildings which exemplify them.

"It is quite the best short history of European architecture that has ever been published in this country."— Herbert Read in the *Architects' Journal*.

"This book admirably introduces an absorbing subject, treated in an imaginative way, which cannot fail to arouse the interest of the reader."—*Studio*.

"This little book deserves to be most warmly commended to all who have a non-professional interest in the history of architecture. It is a marvel of condensation."—*Journal of Education*.